Dionysia Therianou

LEARNING TO FLY

The Kiss of the Spirit

The book is based on real Facts

Therianos Publishing © 2019
Translation: Alexandra Fiada
Artwork: Dionysia Therianos
Cover design: Wendy Pronk
Publisher: Therianos Publishing

Therianos Publishing
Kallithea Zakynthos Greece
Tel : +30 6979113366
Web site : www.therianospublishing.com
Email : therianospublishing@gmail.com

ISBN: 9798680581278

Dedicated to both the born and the unborn souls on this planet

CHAPTERS

The Kiss of the Spirit

My dears men, women, children today that I am writing you this letter, I am an old lady, with long, pure white hair, which I twist into a bun at the base of my neck, and with a thin, delicate face, full of wrinkles. Every wrinkle is the result of knowledge acquired. The deeper the wrinkles, the deeper the knowledge. I am on the short end of 'middle height', but inside me I feel like a giant.

I live at the top of the highest mountain I could ever have imagined.

You cannot imagine either how high it is.

Do you know why? Because it is my mountain.

Do you know where it lies? It lies inside me.

Do you know what it is called?

It is called 'The Mountain of the Soul 'of my soul.

How did I get up here?

It is a story that goes back many years. At times I walked, at times I dragged myself along, at times I crawled, yet at times I flew.

Do you know what's the weird thing about this mountain?

When you have learned to fly, and you have finally reached the summit of the mountain, you lift up your head and you see another peak rising above you.

You fly there. You look around.

You see another peak... and another.

Does it ever end? For me, until now, it has not reached the end.

My dear sister souls, I cannot tell you whether this here peak where I have found myself is a low or a high one, because I do not know the mountain's height.

But I wish to tell you how I got up here.

Maybe, one day, you may also wish to climb up your own mountain, and a thought of mine or an experience, may help fashion for you a feather or even a bit of down. It is enough. Just a tiny feather may become the beginning of the fashioning of your wings.

This is what my granddad used to tell me.

Oh, had you been able to get to know him! You would have loved him, as I loved him myself.

He was such a wonderful person.

I rather look like him as my mirror tells me.

He had a pure white beard and blue eyes. (Mine are green.) His eyes were large, luminous, like the wide seas... They dominated his face.

> *"From a small humble seed,*
> *a huge,*
> *perennial tree may be born.*
> *None of us is insignificant in this world."*

They were so beautiful, serene and limpid.

He would look at you and you would sense him telling you: "I love you, for just what you are. Do not be afraid, I will not judge you. I can clearly see the truth inside you."

You sensed these words of his and so you felt free to recount to him whatever you wanted.

Yet, who was my grandpa?

Why his eyes expressed so much kindness and knowledge? Do you know why?

Because he had also gone up his own mountain. He had created his own wings, strong and beautiful.

And me... But I was still a new-born fledgling.

He wanted to make me fly.

But in order to do so, I had to fashion myself, feather by feather, my own wings.

Grandpa was a healer. He could heal both with his hands and with his mind.

There are so many things I want to tell you about him, that I know not where to begin.

I believe the best would be to start my story at the beginning of our acquaintance when my grandpa and I first met.

I was born in a small village, in a small but, oh so beautiful, is land. My home was a small peasant's house. I was my family's first child and grandpa's first grandchild.

I was born at home. My mother suffered quite a lot in bringing me forth. I had stayed in her belly longer than I should have, and I had been in danger of dying from asphyxiation.

Eventually, after long hours of struggles and agony, I managed to come out into the light of this world.

I was a small and very thin little creature, they were barely able to hold me in their arms.

3

I was at a loss when I came out of Mother's womb perhaps wondering myself how I had managed to escape death and had finally made it.

I did not cry. Not even a whimper.

I came to myself though after receiving a few slaps from the doctor and started crying at the top of my lungs.

The others were laughing, relieved.

As soon as grandpa saw me, he said:

"This child will conquer the world!"

What indeed he could have seen in that small, miserable, weak little creature?

What drove him to say what he said?

One day, I asked him and his answer was extraordinary:

"I saw your soul. This is what you are not your body. The world is inside us. Conquer yourself and you will have conquered the entire world."

And I, as a tiny baby, with all the attention and the love I was receiving, started getting fatter, started growing and becoming a quite pretty, bright child.

I was full of laughter, and I was happy, and all the people around me were glad that I had managed to live.

The previous troubles had by then been forgotten. Life was going on, serene and pleasant.

Until, one day...

"The spiritual trip may start from right this moment
when you are reading this line.
In order to start on your way
you have but to pronounce
the magic word:
I want!"

It was December, on the name day of my father. It was bitterly cold outside. Lots of people had gathered in our house, all sitting around the fire that was burning in the middle of the floor. At that time electricity had yet to come to the village, and the women used to cook on a firepan. They would light a woodfire on the beaten dirt floor of the room, and they would place the cooking pot on an iron tripod.

The whole village would gather to wish "Many happy returns and good ones" to the man having his name day. They were eating, drinking, dancing, singing. It was a day of celebration and joy.

On that day, they had put on the tripod a large frying pan, full of olive oil, in order to fry a kind of sweet pancakes, which were the traditional treat on this particular feast.

They are called "glaoùnes".

These pancakes are made of flour, water, cinnamon, cloves, aniseed and sugar and are fried in very hot olive oil. When nicely browned they are taken out, drenched with honey and sprinkled with cinnamon and sesame seeds. My granny was the one who was making them she was a very capable woman, who had the reputation that she made the best "glaoùnes" in the village. None of the other housewives could make them so tasty. They all suspected that granny had some secret recipe. But she used to say that her only secret lay in making them with love and joy. This is why they came out quite unique in taste.

I loved very much my granny, and I wanted to be constantly with her.

So, on that day I was but fourteen months old and I had started walking I was running, full or merriment, here and there.

At some point, I turned to granny and raised my arms towards her. She lifted me, lovingly, onto her comfortable, plump bosom.

5

Someone called out that the pancakes were burning and granny, bustling about, stood over the frying pan to see how her pancakes were faring.

And then, what was going to be one of the greatest and toughest lessons I had in my life came to pass.

No one understood how it happened and I found myself in the frying pan with the burning hot olive oil.

The right side of my face, half the left side and both my hands were totally burned.

The doctors spoke of a miracle for you cannot have so extensive burns and live.

Yet, do you know which was the even greater miracle? I was not blinded. The entire area around my eyes had been burned, but they were not harmed in the least...

It was inexplicable, they said to my family.

Yet I lived.

Do you want to know how?

Was I happy?

Was I unhappy?

I am going to tell you.

" *Each man comes to Earth for a purpose.*
Find which one is yours.
There are neither great nor small,
important or unimportant purposes.
The purpose of each one of us, whatever it might be,
is the most important thing in the world. "

" Turn the darkness into light!
If you don't succeed in doing so,
it is because you don't wish it.
Certain reasons, that only you know about,
are keeping you in the dark.
Is it guilt?
Is it self-disparagement?
You can find out what it is!
The question is:
do you want to? "

Power of the Will

Until a certain age, I do not remember having a clear idea of what had happened.

However, when I went to school, I realized the extent of the calamity that had befallen me.

There are kids who may mock another even for having an insignificant pimple.

Whatever makes one even a bit different from the majority is food for derision. Colour, dress, behaviour, character, talents, family you name it.

Can you imagine me with the burn damaged face?

Wherever I went there were people who would look at me as if I were a freak. They pointed their finger at me. They pulled faces of pity or disgust.

My skin was red and wrinkled, because, at the time of the accident, in their panic, they had poured water over me. It was the worst possible remedy for a skin that was still being "roasted", when taken out of the pan.

The other kids were calling me "Burned face", "Quasimodo".

They were looking at me as if I were a monster...

I also perceived myself and I felt, too as if I were indeed Quasimodo.

I used to weep day and night.

I could not for the life of me understand how these people could be so cruel to a kid that had never harmed them either by word or deed.

I believe that, sometimes, the grownups were far more cruel than the kids, they would say in my presence whatever came to their mind, without realizing that I have very good ears, a mind able to think, and a soul that could be hurt.

How come, I was thinking, that the soul of a person is unable to understand the pain another soul feels, but try instead to...

I could not find the words to describe how I felt.

I did not know, I was unable to fathom how such a thing could come to pass.

Why would you want to hurt someone else?

What drives you to it?

What kind of pleasure could such a thing offer you?

"Each one of us," grandpa used to say, "creates in this world both his own Hell and his own Paradise."

I had created my own private Hell by the age of six.

It had everything but the kitchen sink in it: tears, sorrow, despair, disaster.

Do you know how is it to believe that your life has been destroyed, before even living it?

Do you know how is it to be afraid to look at people?

To feel that you are not loved?

That you are not accepted as you are?

That you will never be loved?

Do you know how is it to be made fun of?

To be deprecated?

To have your misery taken for granted?

Do you know how is it to have stopped believing in life and in yourself?

"Today focus upon your strength and not upon your
tribulations.
Rise above whatever is happening to you.
You should know that
Man can achieve anything, if he puts his mind to it... "

If you have experienced any of the above, then you will be able to understand, even a little, how I felt.

Each time I was wondering: How come that a person would wish to hurt another one?

Grandpa used to say, "The tongue, my child, has no bones, but it can smash bones".

He would gather me in his large, warm embrace, he would stroke my hair and he would say:

"Do not be afraid!

" Everything that happens in this life, it happens for a reason. Things go past and new ones come, de pending on how you are developing, and depending on what your attention has been focused at any particular time.

" I can see clearly that the time when you are going to fly will surely come.

" All this will go away; and then you will see your own Paradise. It will be the most beautiful, the most wonderful thing you have ever imagined.

" Go forth!

" Let nothing stop you from learning.

" Walk the road of the Worthy Ones and you will see it happen."

He would gently touch the burned side of my face and my tears would drench his hand and his shirt.

He wouldn't say anything else. He would just touch my face and I felt as if he was pouring balm on the wounds of both the body and the soul.

I would stop weeping and would ask him:

"When is this going to happen, Grandpa?"

"When the time comes, my child," he would answer. "When the time comes, nothing can stop it. But everything comes at its own time. It is enough that we are willing it to happen. First of all, however, it suffices to know what we want to happen."

"Oh, Grandpa dear, it is too tough! Will I be able to bear the pain until then? When will the time come?"

"It will come, it will come! You'll see... Have patience, my child!

" Everything will happen at its appointed time. Be strong and it will come. Do not be shy to tell me, always, what is happening to you, what you feel. We are all here for you... You are not alone. We love you very much. We believe in you.

" Keep observing yourself and those who are hurting you. The greatest psychologist is the he who observes himself, his life, the behaviour of other people. Through yourself, you can understand everybody else.

" There is an explanation for everything.

" Do you believe that these who attack you are the strong ones?

" No, my child! They are not, under no circumstances, or for any reason.

" They are just children, who have been hurt by their own family, who seek to project on someone else what they themselves are feeling and what they have received as treatment.

" They do not have the love and the acceptance of their parents they wished for, and this makes them cruel.

"Accept the past, accept the present.
Everything happens for a reason.
No matter how hurtful life's lessons are,
if you choose to turn them into knowledge and power,
you cannot imagine
at what heights they may bring you."

" The isolation or the hate you may experience will heal neither them nor you...

" Only love can change a person.

" Observe what is happening to you and observe the others. This is your defence and your cure."

Grandpa took a deep breath and went on:

"Now, listen to me. I am going to tell you a story about the most humble little creature on Earth. The ant:

" You see, my dearest, the ants exist on Earth for the last one hundred and ten or one hundred and thirty million years and it has been calculated that there are some 22,000 subspecies of them.

" Each subspecies has a different behaviour and way of life. Ants are very intelligent, wise, and supportive of one another.

" Do you know that they have a school for their little ones, in which they are trained as to the task they will be called to undertake in the society where they live?

" Ants are not born programmed to do a specific job, but teachers, in relation with the posts that have to be manned, train them.

" If a little one does not seem to be able to learn, it means that it does not like the specific task, therefore the teachers train it for a different one."

"And what do they train them for, Grandpa?"

"Some of the ants cultivate a kind of fungus, for the sustenance of the nest's inhabitants that is to say, they work as agriculturalists.

" Others raise fleas, tiny caterpillars and other similar insects, since these, because of their diet exude from their bodies a liquid, which is necessary to the ants' diet.

" These insects are kept by the ants as domesticated animals, protected from the elements and from their enemies. In case the tribe moves to another place, these are taken along.

So, the ants that care for them play the role of shepherds. Another kind of ants is warlike, it is constantly at war with other tribes, which they enslave.

" The ant of our story though belongs to a peace-loving tribe, the characteristic of which is great strength. To understand what I mean by this, imagine that these ants can lift a hundred-fold of their own weight.

So, listen to the story of the young ant.

"When you accept the scorn, the ridicule, the torture,

you are ashamed to raise your voice.

You believe that you are to blame,

that whatever is happening to you,

it is happening because, you deserve it.

And yet, the truth is the exact opposite.

The only people who are in need of therapy

– the therapy of love are those who are torturing you."

"The change in your life,
only you can bring it about.
No one else can achieve it for you.
But do you really want to change?
Do you believe in yourself?
Do you love yourself for what it is?
If yes, then never think «I cannot».
Think only:
I am not sure that I can."

The Ant and the Wise Old Man

The ants' colony we are talking about was a rich one, the members of which loved and supported each other very much.

One day, our little ant had gone outside with its parents to gather food for the winter and to transport it to their nest. And while he was going about its business, all of a sudden the sun was obliterated, a dark shadow descended upon him, and he found himself in the hands of a child, who was examining him with curiosity. Almost immediately, the hand threw him into a dark pocket.

The little ant saw light many days later, in an unknown ants' nest.

What had happened?

The child, who took him away, lived in another country. When he arrived at his home, he put the little ant on an ants' nest that existed in the garden of the house.

However, the little ant, by being in the child's pocket, squeezed and moved about, had lost one of his claws and one of his front feet.

So, he found himself in an unknown place, injured and alone.

The ants all around him were busy doing their tasks and paid no attention to the frightened little one.

He found a corner and he slept. He would go outside and eat, but, because of its missing claw, he could not carry food inside the nest.

When winter came, he lived on the charity of the others, who, however, were not always very friendly.

They were pushing him away; they were calling him the 'useless one'.

Yet, where could he go in his condition?

He would weep and lament his bad luck all day long.

He remembered his parents; his friends and he knew he was never to see them again. Daily he was begging for death to come; yet every day he continued to live.

The winter ended, spring came and the little ant went once more outside to find some food.

"The way we see what is happening
to us can change our life forever.
Try, if you want, just for today, to see what has happened
And what is happening, with the eyes of the soul.
For once, set aside reasonable thinking."

One day, when the busy, hurrying ants were pushing him out of their way, all of a sudden, the words of his beloved father came to his mind:

"My child, life is beautiful when we want to make it beautiful.

" Life is life, and it is beautiful only when we live it with strength, dignity, values, love.

" The wilful death and the inaction, the giving up, are cowardice. Stand up straight, no matter what is happening to you, no matter where you are. Remember that you are strong. You can have whatever you desire, provided you wish for it with all the power of your soul."

Then he would take him by the hand and show him the beauty of the world around their nest.

His mother, on the other hand, would caress his face and say with much love: "I believe in you, my dearest child."

The little ant remembered all this and felt that he owed to himself, as well as to his parents, to find the strength inside him. To try and live.

So, he decided to venture into the unknown.

He took to the road and went on and on.

He was almost at death's door from exhaustion when he arrived at an ants' nest very far away. He felt as if these were the last moments of his life.

In a strange way, however, he didn't care, because he was very satisfied with himself having found, finally, the strength to try towards a better life.

At least, he had not given up without a fight. Now, what will be will be, he thought, and let himself lie in the dirt.

He shut his eyes and wrapped himself in a redeeming sleep – which, he thought, was death itself. He awoke up in a warm, friendly nest, filled with food to the rafters. Next to him sat a venerable old ant.

"My child..." he heard the old ant say.

"Am I alive?" he asked.

"You are," he was answered.

The little one recounted what had happened to him, from the very beginning.

And, since that moment, a new life began for him.

The old ant was the wise man of the tribe.

He kept the little one with him, to help him in his everyday tasks and he was speaking to him about life, about the world, about self-awareness, and he was closely watching every movement and every word of the youngster.

One day, the old ant said to the young one:

"Despite the fact that you are a foreigner for us, I will teach you and you will be the next wise man of the tribe, when I will depart this life."

"But I do not deserve such an honour. I am worth nothing. No one wants me. No one takes any account of me. Why would you do such a great thing for me?"

"Because you deserve it more than anyone else. For years I have been watching and searching among our young, in order to decide whom shall I leave to succeed me.

" You have proven to me, but also to yourself, that you have the strength and the will to do it.

"If you believe that you are safe only in isolation,
observe your life.
Do you like it? Then, go on.
But if you do not like it, you should know that
there are many people around you ready to give you a hand.
You need to search and to expose yourself."

" You have tried hard for what you wanted; you did not give up when confronted with difficulties. And although you faced hard ships and insults, you held on to your kindness.

" When I spoke to you on the power of forgiveness and of love, you understood the meaning of my words.

" You forgave those who had insulted you, and you did good deeds whenever you could.

" I was watching you all this time. You have proven to me that there is greatness in your soul, and therefore you will be the next wise man of our tribe."

And so, it all came to pass. Our little ant grew up to become a great wise man, even greater than his teacher. He taught many little ones how to fly.

The ants that have wings are all from the tribe where our little one became wise man.

And, of course, as such, he wrote down the basic principles for the flying lessons of his pupils:

• The first thing you need to know is that: You can fly. You have to want to do it, though.

• The second thing is that: You have every right to fly. There are no restrictions as to who you are, where you come from, or what your age is.

• The third is you should know that: The wings are the positive thoughts, the thoughts of strength, of the love of our self, of the love we have for the others, of the love we have for life. Start constructing your wings, thought by thought.

• The fourth is: Constantly keep on learning and training yourself to become able to fly. Strengthen your wings through your faith to yourself and your potential.

• The fifth is: At any moment, try to fly. Despite the problems and the difficulties, do not forget your purpose.

• The sixth is: If you happen to fall and hurt yourself, do not say, "I give up, I cannot go on", but learn from this experience. Get up, dust your wings and try again.

• The seventh is: To acquire so much assurance and strength that, in any difficulty or reversal, to be able to say: "I know that, one day, I will fly. This is my truth".

• The eighth is: Truth should govern your relationship with yourself. If you feel that today you do not have the courage to fly against a strong wind, wait until it abates.

• The ninth is: To fly high and to enjoy the world from up there without arrogance, without thinking that you are at a higher level than everyone else.

• The tenth is: To aid, with love and humility, others to fly.

"This is what our little ant wrote in his book," said my grandpa, ending the story. "And he lived happily ever after, and so did we even stronger and happier!"

"Today, choose to believe in you.
Look inside you, observe yourself
and find the reasons for which
you deserve to have something like this happen to you.
If for the time being,
you do not consider
that these reasons are enough,
rearrange your life
in such a way as to have reason to love yourself...
You will be generously rewarded for your decision."

Man and Soul

I was listening open mouthed to grandpa and, ever since, I never forgot the humblest of the most humble. Whenever I saw winged ants, I knew that our wise little ant had taught them. "You are fighter!" grandpa would cry at the top of his voice. "Battle on to achieve your wishes. You can do it!"

At that moment I would feel so strong that nothing seemed impossible to me.

Strength flooded both my mind and my body, and it filled my eyes.

I would feel it in my tingling hands, which I had thrown out as if I were ready to fly.

One day, grandpa told me: "The time has come to teach you how to fly."

"How can such a thing happen?" I wondered.

"It will happen. Trust me."

"Grandpa, am I also worthy of flying, just like the little ant you told me about?"

"You cannot yet imagine how worthy you are. We will discover this together you will see."

To fly, I was thinking. How beautiful could that be!

But how?

I knew, the only thing perhaps for which I was sure at that moment, that grandpa did not speak idly.

He said it? That's it.

Life and love for life overflowed from his soul, they were obvious in his bright, tender eyes, were expressed in his words, in the hug he would give you.

"Life is just one thing: the wonderful, fascinating exploration of what life is.

" It takes strength to be an explorer; it takes love for the un-known. Daring!" would grandpa say and open his arms wide, like strong wings, and shout with all the power of his soul, lifting his eyes to the heavens: "Life needs streeeeength!"

He would take me by the hand, show me the overcast sky and I would feel the first raindrops on my wounded face.

The wind was blowing in my hair...

"Look, feel the power of the sky, the power of nature!

" Open your arms and shout:

" 'I am strong!

" I can accomplish anything!

" I deserve to succeed!'"

And I would look at the sky, lift my arms and shout: "I am strong!

" I can accomplish anything!

" I deserve to succeed!"

"Louder!" grandpa would yell. "Ever louder!"

"

"Treat with love the child inside you.

Only you can give it what it needs.

A lot depends on that treatment.

The child inside us defines our behaviour and our beliefs.

Everything is build upon those first foundations.

If they do not lead you towards a happy life, demolish them all!

Keep whatever materials are useful

and build new foundations."

And I would shout, so loudly that I felt the voice coming from the utmost depths of my body.

Deep inside me, an explosion was taking place.

I, the small, hurt human being, was being shattered into an infinite number of pieces.

I was scattering myself all over the earth and the sky.

Each of my pieces was as strong as all the others.

A huge power spread out into pieces of equal strength.

Grandpa would take me by the hand and we would run with all our might through the fields the rain pelting our faces.

"I am free! I am strong! I am able!"

Grandpa was shouting. "I am strong! I am free! I am able!"

I was joining my voice to his.

I would stumble and fall.

"It does not matter," he would tell me. "The important thing is to get up and go on. Come, get up. Let's go."

On the way, we would find wounded birds, kittens and other little animals.

Grandpa would teach me how to heal them.

He would show me how to make a nest with my palms and hold them, keeping them warm within.

"Now look," he would say. "A bright light coming out of your hands and warming the little animal. See the light filling up its body, becoming one with it and making it lively and happy once more."

I could feel the little animal in my hands, trembling from fear, its tiny heart fluttering.

At that moment, I wished so strongly to make it well, that I could clearly see and feel the light issuing forth from my hands, while the love I felt for that little creature was getting stronger by the minute.

I would feel the animal calming down, and I would shut my eyes and visualize it running, once more healthy and happy, through the fields.

As soon as I was certain that it had revived and was well, I would set it free, and it would run away without looking back. I was happy.

Grandpa was watching me, then he would take me by the hand and we would leave, without exchanging a single word.

One day, he said to me, "You are a healer."

"What does it mean?" I asked.

"To heal, my child, in the wise language of our ancestors, means to serve, to repair a damage, to worship, to eagerly occupy myself doing something. The important thing to remember is that the healer is a servant."

"What do you mean, Grandpa?"

"Being a healer does not mean that you are above the others. All people are healers. Some of them, however, remember it and aim at also reminding it to others. We have all come here for a special, unique purpose. We need each other, we complement each other.

Always be humble. When you heal, do it selflessly. You will find inside you the source of love, and it's clear, pure water will be the one you will use to quench thirst and heal wounds both of the body and of the mind.

Grandpa looked deep into my eyes and went on: "All people, we are one.

"We are all different.
We are all one.
Love is healing,
because this is our essence.
We can heal ourselves and each other."

24

Wednesday ✓

Weight ✓

Tommorrow Tommorrow ✗

Although ✓

People ✓   9/10

Actually ✓

Surprise ✓

easant ✓

actory ✓

mpire ✓

” We are all healers of our self and of others.

” None of us is either inferior or superior.

” We are simply different.

” What joins us together is love.

” What separates us is the lack of love.”

"It means, Grandpa, that I heal because I love?"

"This is the only reason, my child. There is no other.

” Many times, we stray into the humdrum of everyday life, and we forget who we are.

” No one has any more the time to stop and think who he really is.

” What has he come to Earth to accomplish?

” Why does he live?

” How does he live?

” What is he thinking?

” What does he want?”

"Grandpa, even you, the grownups, cannot answer these questions either?"

"There are times that we, the grownups, feel that we have lost ourselves in the turbulence of all these things we are label ling 'problems'...

” We do not realize that we are responsible for our future, for the future of our children and for that of the entire humanity.

” We have become the shadows of ourselves.

” We are shadows.

” Imagine how it is to become the shadow of the shadow.”

Grandpa took me by the hand and we went home.

We did not speak until arriving, but I could feel he was sad.

That evening, as I was sitting at his feet in front of the fire place and I was asking him about the things he was talking about, he started recounting a fairy tale.

"The hour of decisions has come.
If you are a child, you should know
that insulting and torturing
those whom you think they are weak
does not make you powerful.
You are just driven by cowardice
and lack of love to behave in this way.
If you are an adult, and you have learned
to assert yourself
through the fear you inspire on others,
learn how to cure yourself.
Do not deceive the children
that such a behaviour
will assure for them a happy and safe life.
Do not procrastinate!
You do not know how long you are going to live.
Do not miss out on the opportunity
to be liberated in this life."

Planet Phaos

Once upon a time, at a distant planet, there lived a kind of people who shone like light.

Their thoughts were beautiful, full of love and kindness.

Their children were born luminous and they learned how they, too, would have luminous thoughts.

It was an extremely beautiful planet.

On it your thoughts became reality.

There was no malice; they knew neither spite nor evil doing.

They all loved each other and they were equal before the law.

They called their planet Phaos.

One day, a huge black cloud, covered the always clear sky of Phaos.

From the cloud descended dark, gloomy people.

They did not carry any weapons, they did not threaten, they did not kill anyone.

But they enslaved the entire population of the planet.

"How did it happen?" I wondered.

Grandpa smiled and went on with the story.

Their submission came in a very simple, yet devilish way, because the Dark Ones became false friends with the Luminous Ones.

And then they started emitting the energy of dark thoughts, saying nasty things, disparaging others, judging others, being violent, wanting to make the others work for them without any remuneration.

And, of course, they were also giving birth to children, who they raised on the principles of darkness.

So, slowly but steadily, the whole planet turned dark.

Then terrible times started reigning on the planet wars, public strife, domestic violence, hate, nastiness.

Man would kill man for crumbs, for a parcel of land, for money, for power.

Love and kindness were considered weaknesses.

"It is possible that our need for the good opinion of others, of their acceptance, of their love, may force us to forget our values, our way of life, even our own self.

The strong ones, the cool ones have accepted us...

We have found a powerful group and we have become members.

We have everything we were thinking we would ever need.

So what?

We are missing out on the chances this life offers."

They became excuses for denigrating or ridiculing someone. Whoever spoke of or acted with love was now considered stupid. And of course, no one wanted to be regarded as stupid.

The few Luminous Ones that had remained believed that there was nothing they could do and let themselves be swallowed by the darkness.

They forgot their previous life.

They were talking and acting like everyone else, in order to be accepted. And their children did the same.

In order to belong to the groups of the strong ones, they were behaving as they did.

So, they lost themselves, because of the fear to deal with a rejection.

Yet, they did not know that the strong people they were admiring, were the greatest cowards they could have imagined...

"But, Grandpa, how such a thing could be done?" I interrupted impatiently the narration.

"You should know, my child, that when you like to torture or to denigrate someone and this act makes you feel that you are worthy and powerful, it means that you have lost yourself."

He caressed my hair and went on:

"The fear you like your presence to rouse, is the heavier, the stronger chain that you could possibly forge for yourself.

" These kids had grown without love and without acceptance.

" Growing up without being accepted for what they were, they became cruel and so they were searching acceptance through fear- the fear they roused in the breasts of both people and animals.

They were unhappy souls, doomed to live their lives in darkness, since they refused to see the light inside themselves."

"And all folks on Planet Phaos were turned into Dark Ones?"

"Yes."

"And if someone was to tell them that they were once Luminous Ones? And that they could become once more like they were?"

"Then, yes!

" One day they would start remembering who they really are and their planet would change once more.

" Yet, who could do such a thing?"

I thought a while.

"A Luminous One, Grandpa.

" Someone who would have pretended to be a Dark One, in order to fool them and then, as soon as he would become strong enough, he would start talking to the former Luminous Ones and remind them who they really are.

" Then, one by one at the beginning, and soon all the more and more, they would make Planet Phaos luminous once more."

"And what of the Dark Ones?

" What would happen to them?" asked grandpa.

I stopped again to think.

I was thinking that they could vanish, that they could go far away.

But then I could see that such a solution did not annihilate the threat that they could return to the planet one day.

What if they killed them all?

But then the Luminous Ones would become Dark.

"Today, lift your eyes to heavens.

Open your arms wide and say:

I love, because I am love;

I can illuminate the world, because I am light.

I acknowledge my real nature.

This is my truth."

Exactly the same as the ones they wanted to chase away. Nothing would ever change...

After sometime I found an answer that satisfied me.

"They would also become Luminous Ones.

" They will be taught love, so that they will be able to see the difference between the light and the darkness and they themselves will choose the light."

"I agree with you," said grandpa. "Your strength lies on knowing who you are and why you are what you are.

" So, you are not in danger by anyone.

" Only in this way Planet Phaos will remain luminous and beautiful.

" Only in this way they will live well ever after and we even better."

"If you regard love as a weakness, then,
at some point in your life,
you will behave to some other person
in the same way that those
who have hurt you behaved towards you.
It is only then that they will have won.
At no other time."

I remember one day, when I was feeling weak and the darkness around me was thickening grandpa speaking to me; and I can hear his words, as if I am hearing them right now:

"Fly to the sky, beyond yesterday, beyond today.

" Go!

" Let your soul gallop unhindered to places unknown.

" Feel the pulse of the Earth inside you.

" Set yourself free!

" Break your chains!

" You do not deserve to be a slave.

" Let your eyes roam freely beyond the horizon, feel the wet sand under the soles of your feet, the wind in your hair and say: 'I am alive, and I like it. I am a human being, and I like it. Life is very beautiful. I can experience many pleasures!"

"Grandpa, what does it mean to be a human being?"

"Well, the time has come," he answered, "to speak to you about our language and about Socrates, the grandfather of all of us. Socrates was a Greek philosopher, who lived between 469 399 B.C. He was one of the great philosophers of ancient Greece. He was an Athenian and one of the most significant personalities of both the Greek and the world civilisation.

" The Greek language is a very meaningful one. This means that a name connotes totally and without any misinterpretation, the essence of what it describes.

" Well, Socrates spoke about the name that denotes us as human beings and which in Greek is 'Anthropos' you heard of 'anthropology', right? He explained the meaning of the word by explaining the meaning of its components. He said all animals – apart from humans do not study the things they see, do not contemplate them and they do not 'anathro'; that is to say, they 'do not observe'. Man, once he sees something in Greek 'opope' something, then he 'anathro' and contemplates what he 'opope'. So, 'anathro a opope' was abridged to 'Anthropos' the Greek nominative takes an 's' at the end of the word.

" Anthropos, that is 'Man', is the one who reflects and judges what he has seen.

" There are also a few other etymological inter predations of the word.

" Also, it is good to know that the Greek language defines man based on man's mental abilities.

" These are some of the things I know and I can tell you about our language.

" Later on, you should search and learn much more.

" Socrates, although he is considered one of the greatest wise men, at the end of his life he said:

'One thing I know, that I do not know anything'.

"The arrogance that we know a lot, because we have read books and we have stored in our memory word for word what has been written, or that we are proficient in a certain knowledge or a scientific field, is the greatest stupidity an educated person can be blamed for, since it is obvious that his education has become sort of 'distorted'.

Socrates said about arrogance:

'The empty goatskins are inflated by the wind and the silly people are puffed up by arrogance'."

"The only reason that I feel different from the others
is because I do not know myself.
The only reason that I am sorry for myself is because
I do not believe in myself."

Ever since, every time I would catch myself being arrogant about something, I would remember Socrates and I would feel like the wind inflated goatskin.

The image itself was enough to deflate me straight away.

Grandpa used to tell me that everyone needs to know about the roots of his people and about his language.

All people are admirable, and so are their languages.

"I want you to get to know your ancestors. This how you are also going to learn about yourself," he would tell me.

He would talk to me about the philosophers and their teachings. He would recite their maxims, first in ancient Greek and then in translation.

I remember once telling him that I was feeling crushed under the burden of the thoughts and the negative comments I was receiving, and I was insisting that he should help me.

But he said: "'Φορτίο μη συγκαθαιρεῖν, αλλά συνανατιθέναι τοις βαστάζουσι.' This, my child, is one of the saying of Pythagoras, who lived in 580-490 B.C. He was a really great philosopher."

"What does it mean, Grandpa?"

"'Do not help people lay down their burden; help them to carry it.'

Each one of us is carrying his burden and the burden is as heavy as he can bear. The heavier the burden, the stronger you are. The stronger you will be. I will always be here to help you carry it."

Grandpa's words were magical.

Years later, I realized that you do not need a magic wand in order to do what you want in your life or in order to help others, aiming to change them there and then.

The greatest magic in the world was the one grandpa cast upon me.

He was teaching me gradually, with love, to build strong foundations, unshakable by either the elements or time.

Oh, my dear Grandpa, oh, were you to know how many times I came to remember your words!

How many times I thought I had broken my wings and I believed I would never fly again!

Yet every time I would heal myself the way you taught me how, and then I climbed upon the foundations you helped me built and, once more, flew away.

Once more overseas, islands, people, deserts, skies...

I would once again open my arms, spread myself to the four winds and let them take me where they wished, riding the untamed horse of my soul.

It was neighing free, in the four-pointed wind and the infinite; it was thirsting to fly, to reach the distant Planet Phaos.

Grandpa turned me into a witch, too.

A witch who never lost her power. She only wanted to forget about it and, a few times, she renounced it.

Grandpa, I went beyond time, beyond space, just as you taught me.

"Time does not exist," you told me. "All these things are creations of our mind, which is unable to comprehend beyond a certain limit.

" Space does not exist either. But we are unable to comprehend it.

" It started as a delusion and in the end we all believed it.

" Do you know, my child, what still keeps this delusion alive?"

"What?" I asked.

"Well, listen to what a fairy tale has to say about it," answered grandpa.

"Today take a deep breath of love
from the ocean of love, in which you float safely.
Look around you those who love you.
Send them a thought of thanks,
for being there for you.
Realize how lucky you are
to have them on your side.
In case you do not have anyone to love you,
seek one out.
There exist in this world
a great many beautiful souls,
who can understand you
and offer you what you desire."

The Soul, the Evil and the Fear

Once upon a time, there lived a beautiful young girl, called Soul. She was flying free through the universe, happy in her own existence. Whatever she touched, it bloomed; whatever she thought of, it was healed.

One day, a malicious, spiteful young man saw her. His name was Evil.

From the moment he saw her, he started chasing her, because he wanted to catch her and enslave her. Soul, however, would always escape him and, always free, she would roam the skies, lifegiving and healing.

Yet the young man was determined to take her as his own.

So, he thought of asking a very good but dreadful friend of his to help him.

His friend was called Fear.

He was invisible and so he could very easily get close to anyone he wished to.

Fear started following free Soul around, getting in front of her, letting her go through him, as she was flying through the air.

He would whisper to her from behind the wind: "Watch out, you are in danger!"

And every time, he would leave something of himself inside her.

It took a long time before Fear managed to conquer this beautiful girl, but in the end he did it and he delivered her, bound in chains, to his friend Evil.

Soul, hypnotized by Fear, succumbed to the will of Evil. His tastes ran to slavery, darkness, pain, sickness, renunciation of life itself, violence, and inability to have dreams and to realize them.

Soul, enslaved and hypnotized, no longer flew around to give the world life, healing, love, beauty and everything was withering away.

"This wonderful Soul is inside us.

She is ourselves.

What has enslaved us?

Who has fooled us and we believed him?

How are we to free ourselves?

Every moment we may find aid around us.

Let us ask people to help us.

We have each other.

This is why we have come in this world all of us together."

Evil was triumphant and, together with his friend Fear, they were boasting of their cleverness.

They were enjoying the dominance over Light and the spreading of Darkness.

Soul had two very good friends: Light and Love. And they had been searching for her all that time.

But they could not find her anywhere.

Because Soul, imprisoned in the dark dungeons Evil had, seemed to have resigned from life and from what she really was.

One day Light, who had not stopped for a single minute to look for her, found a very small crack and slid into the dungeon. He saw her. More beautiful than ever, but asleep.

One of his rays lit her heart.

Love slipped through Light and warmed her up.

And the heart spread the light and the love to her entire being.

And then, the miracle happened. Soul awoke up!

"Grandpa, did she manage to free herself in the end?"

"She did. Do you know when?"

"When?"

"When she realized what had happened.

She saw how Fear had managed to contain her. She looked into her and dissolved all the pieces of Fear that were in there. These were her chains.

She was liberated. And then she realized that she was stronger than any fear.

Evil could no longer find a way to conquer her, because Soul was afraid of nothing.

Just the air generated by her passage, would break him into pieces.

" Yet, instead of blaming herself, that she allowed such a thing to happen, she became stronger.

She now had learned how to be stronger than Fear.

39

So, Fear lost his ability to become invisible and Soul could instantly discern him.

Fear, no matter how hard he was trying to conquer her, he was unable to.

Soul lived free and strong, beautiful as ever, and we are even more free and more beautiful."

The image of wonderful Soul, dressed all in red, riding a beautiful horse raising her hand and stopping Fear by simply looking into his eyes, and then, fearless, going on to gallop through the skies was for me a reminder throughout my life.

"She is your own soul," I would hear grandpa say. "This woman is you.

" Lift your hand and stop fear!

" Do not let anything get in you.

" Find the pieces of your old fears and study them until you overcome them.

" Do not submit in the slavery of fear.

" You deserve to be free, to live.

" Otherwise, you do not live. You only exist."

"Fear exists only because we are unaware

of our potential, of our real nature.

When we will realize this,

we will no longer need fear in our lives."

The Love

My dear Grandpa, I still have the marks from the chains. But you know something?
I only have the marks.
The chains have fallen off. I broke them!
If you only knew how many times I have wept in despair, helpless in my slavery...
I remember grandpa talking to me about his favourite writer, Nikos Kazantzakis, who lived from 1883 to 1957. He would read me excerpts from his books. One that stuck in my mind, said:
"Hey, you poor Man, you can move mountains, you can perform miracles, yet you are sinking in dung, sloth and ungodliness. You are carrying a God, and you do not know it. You become aware of it in the hour of your death, but it is too late."
"Man can really move mountains," grandpa used to say.
"Mountains! But, poor Man, he does not know it. He has forgotten how. Now, instead of moving mountains, he is creating mountains, that rise, huge and menacing, above him and are crushing him."
"What kind of mountains, does Man creates," I asked.
"He knows not who he is.
" He has not observed himself.
" Any disparaging thing he hears about Man, he believes it is true.
" Any bad thing he hears about himself, he believes he deserves it.
" He thinks the life he is living is the only reality.
" He is ridiculing anything that is different from what he believes is the unique and only truth.

” From the moment we are born, we are fashioning the stones and the rocks of our mountain.

” Fears, hates, nasty criticisms, beliefs, dependences, prejudices, smallness of thought.

” These are a few of the stones and the rocks that are crushing us.

” The more they are the higher the mountain we are raising.

Now, listen to a fairy tale.

"Every moment, your thoughts your words,
feed your positive or your negative energy.
You are the one who is creating, each moment,
thought by thought, the links of your chains.
You are not the victim.
You are the manufacturer of the chains.
Take care of it today! Now!
Yesterday does not exist anymore.
Tomorrow has not come yet."

"When you love what you are
and you trust yourself,
no one can humiliate you.
If you give one this power,
then it means that you,
before anyone else does so,
are humiliating yourself.
Stand up straight,
raise your soul's stature.
It is awesome!"

The Love

The Good King and the Wicked Witch

Once upon a time, in a faraway kingdom, lived a king.

He was a very good king and a brave one. None could vanquish him in battle.

He was ruling with kindness and love, and everyone in his kingdom was happy. He never went to war in order to conquer, only when it was necessary to defend himself.

No one, ever, had managed to enslave his country.

In a neighbouring kingdom ruled a crafty, warmongering king, who wanted to conquer the good king.

But all the battles he had given to that end, he had lost.

He was livid with rage.

One morning, he called his councillors and told them that it would be off with their heads, if they would not find a way to get his wish. He gave them until next dawn to do it.

Totally frightened, they were thinking all day and all night what to do.

Dawn was arriving when one of them said:

"I got it! Listen, this is what we will do: we will send the next-door king the wicked witch, transformed into a beautiful princess, along with wagons full of precious gifts for his majesty. After that, she will do everything as it should be done."

And indeed, so it happened.

The incredibly beautiful witch presented herself to the king and offered him the precious gifts. She praised his valour and his kindness, which were renowned even in her faraway country.

And this was why she had travelled, she explained, so far. Because she had wished to meet him.

The king was dazzled by her beauty and by the excellence of her false words. He fell in love with her and asked her to become his wife. She accepted, of course, immediately, and the wedding took place with great ceremony and many feasts.

The witch, from the moment she married him, started working on her evil scheme.

She was badmouthing yet professing love everybody and everything.

She would find fault in anything the king did or said. For his own good, as she would tell him, and from love, so that she would aid him to better himself.

"There are so many beautiful people
around us, who can help us!
The only thing needed is to believe it.
Then we will see that everything is changed."

He started believing that he was not worthy of the woman he loved.

He would get angry with himself and with his loyal, beloved men around him.

They could all see what was happening; but he, blinded by love, would go against anyone who would tell him something different from the one he believed to be true.

It did not take long for him to fashion the mountain that crushed him.

The witch was ready to give the signal to attack the now weak king and bring about the certain occupation of his king dom.

But then, one morning, when the king, crushed by the weight of his burden, was sitting in his garden, a woman, dressed in white and so beautiful that he had never seen the like, appeared before him.

She touched lovingly his head and said:

"Dear King, I am the good witch. All your wife is telling you are lies. Your wife is a wicked witch, sent by your enemy to enslave you. You will unmask her, if you prick the middle finger of her left hand with the crown on the royal ring you are wearing."

The king hurried to go and do as he was told.

And then his wife turned into the more than ugly witch she really was!

The king lost no time: he drew his sword and cut off her head.

The king, when he got over the first shock and saw how badly he had dealt both with himself and his kingdom, by let ting himself believe all the nasty things he was being told, left the palace, dressed as a beggar, and started roaming his country, begging for a little bread.

For months he was travelling from village to village, going uphill and down dale. His feet got sore and wounded, his beard grew long, his body got dirty.

Yet his soul cleared up completely.

One day, sick, short of breath from the hardships he had endured, arrived at a house, high up on the mountains.

A young maiden came out to meet him. She led him inside, supporting him.

The maiden lived in that house, along with her parents and brothers. They all treated the sick beggar as if he were a king.

The maiden healed his wounds, cleaned him up, and spoke to him with sweet words that were balm to his soul.

She was a pretty maiden, but the great beauty of her soul overshadowed any physical beauty.

The king fell in love with her, and she with him not knowing who he really was.

"And, naturally, in the end they got married," concluded grandpa, "and they lived happily in their kingdom for many years. And we lived even happier thereafter."

"Physical beauty is always desirable.
But is it enough?
At some point, it will fade.
Then what's left?
Is it perhaps that the light and the love
that grow inside us day by day,
are our everlasting, incorruptible,
true beauty?"

"Grandpa, did the king tear down his mountain?"

"The king dissolved even the tiniest stone from the mountain, he himself had raised."

"Did the maiden's love help him?"

"Love is the greatest power in the world.

" Love makes you grow tall, grow strong and brave and so go on in life.

" Love can breach mountains, barriers and boundaries."

He caressed my hair.

"Listen to me well," he went on. "The real love of the soul liberates.

" You need patience and will in order to find it. But you need first to cleanse yourself and get to know it.

" To become what you are: Light.

" Then you will understand what freedom means.

" You need to love yourself, for exactly what it is and never let anyone diminish you for any reason.

" Never give anyone that right.

" If you let such a thing happen, you are lost.

" See clearly who you were, and become what you really are, before being crushed by your mountains.

" To say 'I am' and to be indeed.

" To let the other one free, to be.

" Only then you will become the eagle who is flying free in the sky.

" It is then that you will meet the other eagle, who is also flying free.

" Fly next to each other. Look into each other's eyes with strength, love, light the light that illuminates your souls and your world. None of you depends on the other.

" It is then that you can reach God."

49

Myself, when I grew up, I was often projecting on the others what each time I thought I wished them to be. For how long, however, could the other person play the role I wanted him to play?

Inevitably, at some point, he would tire and then he would become himself.

Would I be pleased with this new image?

No.

And this was happening because it was I who wouldn't accept myself as it were.

Yet it was very convenient to me to be able, at any given moment, to blame someone else for what was happening in my life and how it was developing.

It was the safer thing not to be responsible for either my deeds or my words.

There was always someone else who was changing my life, my decisions, my choices.

Until, one day, I realized the game I was subjecting to both the others and myself.

It was very hard to understand it, but eventually I did it.

In reality, it took me a lifetime.

Yet, somewhere inside me, the words of grandpa were lurking, and they were whispering to me all the time:

"You are solely responsible for what is happening to you.

"It is only with love, only with self-awareness
that you can live happily with someone else.
When the need to be with someone else
Is the result of selfishness,
then we have what, unfortunately, happens
all too often among couples and families."

You, and only you, are determining the script of your life, the people who act the parts that you, and only you, are ascribing to them.

" Do not hold them accountable for it.

" Do not ask them to explain themselves to you why they are what they are.

" They are.

" You are.

" But, are you the mask or your real self?

" Take off the mask you are wearing, so that the others will take theirs off, too.

" Look: just like this!"

Grandpa pretended to take off an imaginary mask.

"You do it, too," he would say.

I made the same gesture.

"Which mask is the one you have removed?" he would ask.

I was looking, round-eyed my hands. Couldn't see anything.

"Now shut your eyes and tell me what you see. The first thing that comes to your mind."

"Sadness," I would tell him.

"Why?"

"Today the kids at school where taunting me for my face. They were calling me monster, stupid, worthless."

"And what did you answer them?"

"Nothing."

"Good. Come with me."

He would take me by the hand and the warmth of his palm would bring tears to my eyes. I could feel them stream down my cheeks. I could taste their saltiness. I could feel the pain in my heart, on my face.

We would go out in the rain. Tears and rain mingled. Grandpa would drop to the ground that had already become muddy and would and roll over.

He would make a ball of wet soil and ask me:

"What is this?"

"Soil," I would answer.

He would constantly change the shape of that clay ball, make it take human forms, and each time he would ask:

"What is this?"

"Soil," I would answer.

He took off a golden chain he was wearing and wrapped it several times round the small clay ball.

He asked me the same question.

"Soil," I answered.

"I want you to remember that, no matter what your form is, physical beauty disintegrates.

" Changes.

" Dries out with the years.

" Cracks.

" No matter what riches you were to pile on you, around you, you cannot change anything.

" Certainly, we wish to be beautiful, to be liked and to be admired for it. It is quite healthy and we need to keep our body in a very good physical condition. We respect this wise body, which if you were to study it you would realize that it is worthy of your admiration, because it is our vehicle through this life. Together with it we live our experiences on Earth, we rejoice and we live. By maintaining our vigour through exercise, we are also aiding our spirit.

> *"The world is as you wish it to be.*
> *Do not complain of your life.*
> *It is your choices*
> *that have brought you to this moment.*
> *If you do not like it, change it!"*

" At the same time, however, we need to remember the truth of the essence.

" That which, unaltered and pure, transcends time. That, which lifts us up.

" That which, always weightless, flies in the universe of truth.

" This is the one you should seek and find, no matter how long it will take you.

" Do not care about time; time is false. At some long for gotten moment we invented it because we needed it as a virtual point of reference.

" Real time does not exist; it is a trap to hinder your development.

" As you are growing up, you will be seeing, and realizing, how much the people have been trapped in the snare of space/time.

" This principle we are all adhering to, is a way to control us.

" If you wish to, you will learn everything, otherwise you will remain in your entire life a ball of clay, beautifully shaped and decorated.

" You will be preening yourself, and you will have eyes only for your beauty and your riches.

" So, you will never see your wings. You will never fly.

" Let others try and control the Earth.

" They will never be able to control you.

" The balls of clay cannot reach you up there where you will be. They are stuck on the Earth, in the mud.

" Fly, fly high, my beloved!"

He would smear his clothes, his hair, his face with mud, and he would tell me:

"Come!"

I would stand motionless.

"Mom will reproach me if I get dirty. This is not right, it is wrong."

"Since your decision and your action do not harm anyone, you do it. It's good for you."

Hesitantly at first, I put my feet in the mud. Then my hands. I lifted some mud with my palms and spread it over my face. "Man is made of mud," grandpa said. "Feel your shape!"

Feeling totally free, I would roll along with him on the ground, laughing.

After rolling in the mud, I would go take a bath.

My mother would not believe in her eyes the first time she saw me. Eventually she got used to it.

The amazing thing was that every time, along with the mud, I would also feel washing away from me other, invisible things. I was being liberated through that.

I felt lighter.

It was a kind of revolution, of freedom from what you are not allowed to do.

It was my contact with mother earth.

"Life is beautiful, when you offer to yourself
all those things that make it feel happy.
Give to yourself joy, laughter, life, love.
With respect towards yourself and towards
the others, take the road
on which everything you need in order
to live happily is expecting you.
Know that your happiness does not deprive
anyone of anything.
On the contrary, it adds both to you and to the whole."

You were right, grandpa. Man is made of soil.

What is it that turns him into such a wonderful being? What is it that changes him?

What is it that transmutes him into something we still do not know what it is, what is it that endows him with infinite possibilities? We still do not possess enough knowledge in order to be able to understand ourselves.

Yet I have searched a lot.

I believe in Man, grandpa, just as you did.

It took me a life time to realize it. But it is never too late for anything.

As long as I am alive, I learn, I develop just as you were telling me, dearest grandpa.

One day, grandpa said to me:

"I want you to write the story of your life as a fairy tale."

"Now?"

"Right now. Take pen and paper. Write without thinking."

"I have no idea how to start."

"Start with 'once upon a time'," he advised me.

*"All the riches of the world
and all the admiration
for your beauty will not give you happiness.
Believe that you are worthy.
Because you are you
and you love what you are.
Only then you will feel
the happiness that you have not
known until today."*

The Girl Who Vanquished Evil

Once upon a time, there lived a very evil warlock.

He would roam the world and harm as much as he could the kindest men, the strongest, those in which he could see inside them the brightest light.

He wanted to vanquish good on Earth.

So, one day, as he was aimlessly wandering, he saw the birth of a girl. The light shone around her! And the evil warlock immediately understood what he should do.

"I'll break you!" he decided. "You will not be able to show your face anywhere in this world. The light inside you will become darkness, and you will be transformed into a repulsive creature: a bride of hate and evil. Just another wicked witch in the realm of darkness."

And so, it came to pass. Fourteen months after the birth of the girl, a great fire broke out in the house and it seriously burned the little girl.

It was a miracle that they managed to save her in the last minute.

She lost her parents.

She was raised by an evil aunt, until she sent her back to her ruined house to live by herself.

She repaired it as much as she could, so she would have a roof over her head.

Repulsive to see from her burns, she was growing up in sorrow and rejection.

Tears, pain, anger were her companions. She hated herself, the people, her destiny.

She would hide by day and she would go out by night to gather her food.

She was still very young, but she did not understand it. There was no life for her.

A winter night she heard a knock at her door.

She went to answer it and a man, icy cold like the wind that was blowing out side, pushed her aside and entered.

"I will give you back your beauty, if you become my servant," he told her.

"Who are you?" she asked.

"It is certain that you were not
born to be unhappy.
Anything can happen in this life,
in a magical way.
Be clear on what you want to be.
Focus on that."

"I am the greatest warlock in the world. I will make you my queen, if you agree to fight on my side against the good. Together we will be able to win. No one will distress you anymore; everyone will bow in front of you. You'll have all you ever wished for. I will come tomorrow night for your answer."

He left, disappearing into the icy darkness.

The girl was left deep in thought.

She would become beautiful once more, she would be loved. She would have everything she wished for. The only thing the warlock wanted was to fight against love. That was easy for her. Herself, she had no love at all.

Better not to see it around her it hurt.

Despite the cold, she ran to the mountain that she loved so much.

Just as she realized what she had thought, she stopped.

She had thought the word 'loved'.

Therefore, inside her, she could love?

She thought of the decrepit old woman, to whom she used to take food secretly at night, so that she wouldn't starve. She remembered the shining sun, that caressed her wounded being, and the joy its warmth gave her. She would shut her eyes and its light would spread inside her. She remembered her heart achieving serenity. She saw herself watching, stealthily, the games and the laughter of children, and to laugh along with them. She saw couples in love, seeing the love shining out of their eyes, and being happy along with them.

Walking, lost in her thoughts and her images, she reached the top of the mountain. She knew well every stone of the slope, so her steps did not falter even once in the darkness, in the trail she was following.

There she saw a bright, strong fire illuminating the entrance of a cave.

Something beyond her drew her there.

She walked up to the cave.

An old man was sitting on the ground in front of the fire, warming himself.

He looked at her and he smiled welcoming her.

She smiled in return.

"Come and sit down," he told her.

She sat beside him to get warm. It was nice.

"Are you coming from afar?"

"Perhaps from the end of the world. From the brink of the precipice."

She recounted her story to the old man, not even realizing why or how.

The old man nodded and said:

"It is your decision to choose what to do. Stay here tonight and in the morning, you can tell me what you wish to do. But any way, you should know that the fact that you have arrived here is not by chance. You have the opportunity, perhaps for the last time in your life, to choose between the easy road of the evil and the difficult road of the good."

All night, sitting by the fire, the girl was thinking.

In the morning she had taken her decision:

"I wish to nurture love, kindness, light, forgiveness, beauty. I choose the good."

"If you believe that you are light,

then you can live only as light.

If you believe that you are darkness,

then you can live only as darkness.

The choices you have are very simple:

Am I light?

Am I darkness?"

LEARNING TO FLY | Dionysia Therianou

"Then come with me."
He took her in front of a mirror.
"What do you see?" he asked her.
"Ugliness," she answered.
"Every day you will look in this mirror and you are going to say: I am beautiful!
" I am light!
" I am love!
Never mind if you believe it or not. The day will come, when you will believe it."
They would go out, she and the old man, to gather healing herbs, to makes unguents for her face and body, and they were talking about many beautiful things.
The girl would stay for hours under the bright sun.
She learned how to forgive.
"This is the beginning of everything," the old man would tell her. "Strong people understand, they forgive. Cowards hate, they seek revenge. Choose what you want to be. But do it having total awareness of your choice.
" If you will not be able to forgive, even the one whom you believe did you the most harm, you will never be free and happy.
" Always something will be eating you, day in and day out, in order to nurture itself and continue to live."
Day by day, the old man was teaching her how to live. He was teaching her how to see everywhere beauty, love, light; how to hope.
He was teaching her to love herself for what she was and for what she had achieved in becoming.
Every evening she would thank herself for everything she had done, even if it were a tiny little step.
She learned to heal herself, but also anyone else who had her need and asked it of her.

Time went by. Summers and winters. The girl lived in a timeless time.

One day, as she was saying in front of the mirror:
I am beautiful!
I am light!
I am love!
She saw and felt the light shining inside her and around her.
She believed it.
She was, at long last, free to be herself.
She loved herself.
The miracle had happened.

She was now strong, afraid of nothing. She wanted to fly to places no one knew and to live the unknown and the adventure. There was so much beauty around her, which, before, she had been unable to see.

She thanked the wise old man, who was but the opponent of the evil warlock, and left full of joy to take up her new life.

She would heal people wherever she would go, with herbs and with love.

She lived happily and full of joy her life and we lived even happier and joyful ever after.

"There are no ugly people.

Only ugly images about our self.

See,
believe,
say,
what you really are:

I am light!

I am love!

I have beauty!"

"Because she became beautiful?" asked grandpa.

"Because she loved what she was, as she was.

I know very well, Grandpa, that no matter how often people tell you that you are beautiful, you are never going to believe it, unless you personally have said it to yourself. Unless you personally appreciate your gifts, your talents, you see the beauty your eyes have, you see the beauty of your soul."

Oh, grandpa, after so many years, I have now learned my lesson: People are beautiful all of them and they all deserve to love themselves. When we are kids, we ask our friends or our elders whether we are beautiful.

The answers we are getting depend on the likes and dislikes of each one.

Always in this world there are and there will be people more beautiful or less beautiful than our self.

It is not possible to be liked by everyone, just as we do not like everybody.

If, however, we accept what we are, we do not need anyone else's acceptance.

We need of course to have high moral values and to be fully aware of the truth about our self.

We can be happy.

Otherwise, we will be seeking a life through the others and we will wait for the moment when they will accept that we are the most beautiful, the best kids in the world, in order to become happy and to appreciate our self.

This cannot be done. This is gaol.

Only when we disentangle our self from these needs, we will be able to see our beautiful soul reflected in our face, in accordance with what we are thinking, saying, doing.

This is the real beauty.

"What was that woman at the beginning?" asked grandpa. "Darkness."

"Define darkness."

"I shut the eyes of my soul and I can no longer see the light and the love."

"What did the woman manage to become? What truth did she see?"

"She saw the light and the love."

"Where are they?"

"Always there, and they wait for us to return to them, to open our eyes to see.

" It is us who draw away from them, not they from us."

Grandpa stood up and gave me a kiss.

"You will become a writer," he told me.

"No matter how long it will take you to become one, never forget that you have the talent and the soul to achieve it.

" No matter how many reject your work, no matter how many disappointments will come your way, in those difficult times remember my words.

" One day you will succeed."

Grandpa kept my fairy tale and he gave it to me what I was grown up enough, and had long ago forgotten it.

I still have it.

The paper has yellowed with time, some letters have faded, but it reminds me that I always knew the truth and that for a space in my life I had forgotten it.

Grandpa knew what he was doing by keeping it and giving it to me so much later.

Many times, in my life I have shut my eyes, refusing to see the others and myself.

Alone in my cave, I was fashioning heavy stones and I was building impregnable fortresses.

Seeking what?

Protection from the others.
Yet in the end, I understood a fundamental truth.

*"In real life there is nothing
that separates one man from another.
Only the lie that is created by fear,
and the abandonment of the quest for truth."*

"You should know that when you want

to hurt, denigrade,

harm someone the only one you are hurting is
yourself.

You are frightened and you thirst for love and
acceptance.

You need to understand that the fear you inspire in others

is not the spring where you could slacken your
thirst.

You will never achieve it in this way.

Do you believe, however, that this is what you
deserve to be?

Nothing better?

Nothing higher?"

The Cruel King

Once upon a time, lived a very cruel king. Were you to see him, you would say that this indeed was a very strong man, who was standing squarely on his two feet.

Yet, were you to observe him closely, and were you able to see inside him, you would have seen a small, frightened child, who was sitting curled up, hugging his knees, in a dark corner of the castle he had built inside him.

That king was boasting that he was fearless and brave.

He would kill, by just saying a single word, whoever did not obey his commands.

He believed that he was infallible, and that only he knew what was right therefore whoever dared have a different opinion, he was gaoled or killed.

He was building strong, impregnable castles.

His only worry was his enemies who were lurking out there. Love could not sneak into his castle.

Love was his greatest enemy.

Life was unbearable for his subjects, but for his councillors, too, who lived every day in fear that, may be, by night their head would have left their shoulders.

The king was cruel and unfair.

He never forgave anyone.

One day, the councillors got together.

"We cannot take this kind of fear anymore," they said. "We do not know if the next minute we are going to be alive or dead. We have to do something."

They all agreed that something should be done.

Yet, what would that be? None would venture a solution. They were thinking for days, when one of them said:

"I thought of something, but it is very dangerous and if it fails, we will all die."

"Tell us," said the others.

"Living in fear is no life. At least, let us try to change it."

"If you cannot see the light today,
just think this:
why should there be only darkness?
What is really happening to me
and I insist
on shutting my eyes?
What has hurt me in the past?
What is hurting me now?
What I am afraid of?"

"Hear me then. One day, while I was just sitting and thinking what could possibly be done with the king and, having no idea, I started doodling on a piece of paper, not realizing what I was doing. When at some point I looked at what I drawn, I saw that the shape looked like a sun. I thought of counting its rays. They were eleven. Do you know what is the meaning of this number when it appears randomly?"

The councillors knew quite well that this number symbolized the way of the soul.

The number would appear when you would be ready to leave behind you a life that was bringing you neither joy nor fulfilment, to show you that you were on the right track.

It was as if the number was telling you "Here you are. Go ahead!"

It is up to you to follow the new track, or to be afraid of change and go back to your old path.

Solutions always come, when we seek them and when we leave our mind at peace for a while, so that it can hear the soul.

"Next month, on the eleventh, said another, "it is the king's birthday. It is his chance for a new life. How could this be done, though? Certainly not by talking to him about all this. He will cut our throats as soon as hearing the first word."

"Then," said the man who had told them about the meaning of 'eleven', "we are going to do it without saying a single word. In total silence. Many times, silence is all the words there are. Its power is greater than arguments that have no meaning for the other person. We all have inside us the inner wisdom to know what is best for us."

He explained to them his plan.

And they followed it.

"It is worth fighting against all odds in order to free yourself from fear. You can only gain from it; otherwise you won't be living at all.

You will just be thinking that you are living," they all agreed. So, during the night, they abducted the king from his bed and, through a secret passage, known only to them, they brought him and incarcerated him in an underground, dark dungeon.

They left him there, all alone, with just some bread and water.

The all-powerful king found himself powerless, gaoled, trembling with fear, not knowing what to expect.

He no longer held at his hands the life of others, but certain others were dominating his own life.

In the darkness, his fears started taking shape.

He was screaming, feeble and frightened at times begging, at times threatening asking to be saved.

No answer.

No one.

After a few days he realized that no one would want to save him, because he had not loved and saved anyone himself.

He started contemplating his past and his actions, at the time when people were begging for mercy and he would condemn them.

He remembered the hungry ones, who were begging for food and he would kick them away.

Now it was he who was hungry. Now it was he who was at the mercy of certain others.

"The answers we get
depend on the questions we are asking.
If we are no longer
satisfied with the answers,
the only thing we can do is
to change the questions."

He reflected on what he had been doing. His entire life passed before his eyes and he started weeping bitter tears.

He saw his other self, a totally different man than the one he thought was the real one.

Where had he been hiding that other man all this time?

If he survived this ordeal, he would redress every injustice he had perpetrated.

But, would he survive?

One day, the door of his cell opened.

The king could neither see nor hear anything.

He started begging that man who had opened the door to listen to him.

He started talking to him about his fears, about his life, about all the things he had now understood.

No answer was forthcoming.

The king was asking whether that man, who stood there, understood him, whether he thought he was right but nothing, not a whisper.

This went on for days. The king talked and talked. The other listened. Just listened.

One day before his birthday, the king felt burden free, joyful.

He no longer cared what would happen to him.

He had cleansed his soul. He could die in peace.

He said to the darkness: "I see the light inside me being so bright that it illuminates this cell. I forgive myself and I want to make restitution. I have lived many years of my life in ignorance and fear. Misfortune, arrogance, fear were my daily death. But no longer. I want to live. I have understood that the people around me are a blessing. Each one furthers the other's development."

The same night, the king found himself in his bedchamber. The next day he celebrated his birthday and for years everyone was commenting on the kindness and love with which he was governing his kingdom and received strangers. He lived a happy life, together with the woman he fell in love with and married and with their children, and we also lived even happier ever after.

"Acknowledge the struggle you have been through
in order to arrive where you are today.
Nothing was gifted to you,
nothing was granted.
You did it because you wanted to.
Because you fought with all your might,
and even with resources you didn't know you had.
Give thanks to yourself for this.
Your self deserves it."

The Transgression

One day, I asked grandpa:

"Does 'I fly' mean that I am alone?

" That I leave the others behind?

" That I do not care for them and I look after myself only?

"No," he answered. "It means exactly the opposite. Only when you feel good and free you can be your real self. It only then that love for you and for life flows unhindered. Only when you love, and you are happy with yourself and your life, you can also love the others.

" Then the others do not represent for you a number of responsibilities and a hindrance towards the things you want to experience, but they are your allies in happiness.

" It all depends on how you see things. With the eyes of a free soul or with the eyes of a caged self, who sees wrong choices everywhere, as well as tiresome obligations that are the result of those errors in judgement?

" If this is the case, then you are reduced to a continuous and unchecked hypnotic state.

" You constantly feel that you want to sleep in order to rest.

" You will never find rest, however, as long as you are tiring your own self.

" The decisions are always yours.

" No one can save you from this thing; only you can save yourself.

" You will need lots of strength.

" You will need to transcend yourself.

" The reward, once you achieve it, is priceless and immediate."

Life has proven to me beyond any doubt what grandpa was telling me that day.

When you follow this road, miracles happen.

Things have happened to me, which I had never dreamed I would experience them.

Following every 'thank you' I would say to myself, every acknowledging of its power, every transcendence I would make, things happened and they were all magical, perfect.

I finally became aware that me and only me I am responsible for my way of thinking and for my way of life.

In the place of every old negative thought, I would put a new one, of positive strength.

The old one would insist; but so would I with the new one.

I refused to give up, until I had conquered the automatic reactions.

So I came to conquer unknown areas, castles that had seemed impregnable and the reward was great.

Wonderful people would appear on my path, people who wanted to help make my dream come true.

All over the world I met countless beautiful people. This, for me, was the greatest blessing.

Each time, these wonderful souls of light and of love made me stronger, freer even if only by their presence.

"As long as we are carrying in our mind
the people who have hurt us, those who made us angry,
we cannot be free.
Every day we are going to tighten the noose at our throat,
believing that with this we are harming them.
We are going to be self-strangled."

Even when I will be on my deathbed, I will continue thanking and being grateful to that higher power from which I have issued. Myself, who managed to make it. The wonderful people in this world.

I can say, with a soul full of joy, that I am happy!

We are not alone.

On day, the teacher at school asked us:

"What would you like to become when you grow up?"

When my turn came, and before I had a chance to answer, he laughed scornfully and said: "Teacher?"

The other kids laughed.

I did not speak at all.

When I went home, quite distressed, I told grandpa what had happened.

"It doesn't matter what they think of you. And don't you think that the grownups always know the truth either about the others or about themselves. Were they to know it, they wouldn't say such things to children. So, forgive your teacher, because he does not know what he should know, and go on," said grandpa.

"It is necessary, of course, and for you, on your part, to be fully aware that the others see only what we believe at that particular moment about our self and our abilities. This observation will help you answer, each time, a few crucial questions, which only you can answer.

" What do you believe that you are?

" What do you wish to become?

" What is your vision?"

"To become a writer."

"Do you want it very much?"

"I think so. But, perhaps, what if I am not worthy enough? Is, maybe, this dream too grandiose for me? How can I achieve it?" I asked, full of anguish.

75

"One day, one of his pupils asked Socrates," started grandpa, in his storytelling voice.

'Master, how shall I manage to achieve what I want in my life?'

" Near them there was a barrel full of water. Socrates all of sudden, grabbed his pupil by the hair and, with all his strength, pushed his head into the water, keeping it under until he knew that the young man could no longer hold his breath. Only then he pulled his head out of the water. Feeling faint, but also angry, the young man asked Socrates why he did such a thing. 'You will achieve what you want, when you will want it as much as your breath,' said Socrates. This is the answer," said grandpa finishing his story.

Many times, later in my life, I remembered Socrates.

For years I had been trying to publish my book, without any success. The rejection slips were arriving the one after the other. I would hear and read disdainful comments by the dozen. Once, I went to a friend of mine and asked him to help me with his advice, since the world of books was familiar to him.

He asked to read it, so he could give me some aid with the text. We agreed that, the next time I were to go to his office, he would give me the telephone numbers of a few publishing houses. Full of joy and trust, I left my book in his hands.

I was feeling as if that book was my child. For me, this was very important.

I was in agony waiting to hear what he had to say.

"If you are experiencing failure
in something you wish very much,
seek and find the fears
that have the power to stop you."

After a few days, when I went to see him, I got his answer.

Sitting behind his desk and looking severe, he almost threw the book in front of me, declaring that he did not like it in the least and that he would never aid in the publishing of such a thing.

He gave me no advice whatsoever and, certainly, no publishers' telephone numbers.

After the initial shock, I acknowledged the great lesson on accepting criticism by others.

He had every right to his opinion, and for me it was an important lesson: to accept and to respect criticism.

It is a prerequisite for someone such as a writer who is constantly exposed to it.

Unless you are ready to accept criticism, you cannot go on. Later in life, I often mentally thanked that man, who had the strength to teach me that very hard lesson.

This happens every minute in our life.

Sometimes lessons are hard; they hurt us.

But if we see beyond that, everything changes.

What has the thing that is happening to me to teach me? Into which unknown areas is it leading me?

On which aspect of my being is it making me stronger?

Towards what does it develop me?

Which fears does it force me to face?

Another time, I found myself talking with a publisher, to whom I had given my book to read.

"Why should I publish your book?" he asked me. "You are unknown. I have very powerful writers from abroad, dealing on the same subject, who have made the bestsellers list. What value can you have? I want to have sure sales."

"Because in the hands of God, all implements have the same value," I answered. "Even the humblest, the smallest, which appears totally insignificant, is important in the creation of the end product in God's work."

Often, I would give it all up, disheartened, trying to forget my great dream.

Then I would get up and start all over once more.

And the years were going by.

One day, I decided to face the truth. I had enough.

"Why doesn't it become reality, since I want it so much?"

Grandpa's question came to my mind, whether I wanted it to happen, and the story of Socrates and his pupil.

I had learned not to hide myself from the truth, and so I had to admit that I did not want it as much as I did my breath.

Yet, why didn't I want it?

Because I was afraid to expose myself.

I was afraid that I would be ridiculed, that I would be judged inadequate for the task. The comments I had heard in the past were repeating themselves in my mind, stronger and more often, than the will to do what would make me happy. I could see those kids and the grownups of the past making fun of me, as when I was a child.

I preferred inaction to having to face a possible failure. From whichever side I was looking at it, I would come against some fear, which was stopping me.

"Every morning that you open your eyes to the new day,
remember what you want to do.
Which is your aim today?
Say: Today a new road is opening up for me.
I can see it clearly.
Today I consciously choose the good,
because I know that I cannot be anything else but that."

I also saw clearly some of the reasons I wanted the book to be published for reasons that were requiring thought and treatment.

Through that wished for success, I was seeking the acceptance I did not have as a child.

The child inside me was still bitter, angry.

I wanted to become famous, to show them who I am.

Yet, what kind of happiness comes through fame?

What does it matter if other people recognize you, while you are still carrying inside you anger and an unhappy child?

Have you succeeded?

Is it happiness?

Not to me.

On the contrary, it is too dangerous.

You are in danger to miss forever your chance and your road.

To turn yourself into a goatskin full of air, which will be carried away by the wind and will be lost in the wrong paths.

You are in danger of thinking that this makes you different, exceptional that you are someone.

The most important: you will miss the opportunity of getting to know your real self and all the things that are worth knowing and experiencing in this life.

It is possible that, at some point, the wind may stop blowing and then you, hanging in mid-air, you will be deflated and you will be killed, falling from that height.

I did not believe that I deserved that great dream. I acknowledged all these. I saw them clearly.

And so, I set other solid foundations, not for the purpose of climbing onto a pedestal, but for flying. In order to express the truth and the love from love and not for any other reason.

No matter what would happen, I was doing what I loved most. Write.

Then everything started changing.

Do you know which magical thing I saw in life?

That the cure, when the time comes, arrives through exactly the same conditions. At that time it seems incredible, but it is the truth.

Just as that friend of mine, that first time, rejected my book, when the time was right, many years later, another friend, who was working in the same field, did her best to help me publish it.

It does not matter how much you can give the other person to help him realize his dream.

A small word, a small offering, when the other needs you, can create miracles.

Yet, why things changed for me?

Because by now I was certain that this was my purpose and that I was totally capable of being successful.

Now, I was strong inside myself. Nothing could daunt me; nothing could side-track me from my point of focus.

I am worth it!

My book is worth publishing.

I was flying...

Now everything on my path was coming to help me achieve my goal.

"We can achieve anything.
This is the truth we need to know.
With respect,
with love,
with light
we are taking our dreams in our hands
and we are giving them breath through our own breath."

Everything, but everything, may be achieved, when you heal with your love the child inside you. When you love it and make it feel safe, so that it will come out into the light.

The child fights back, because it is afraid.

The child believes that it is not capable of anything; it is not strong enough in order to make it.

With your love, with your total acceptance of what the child is, you will succeed using the words that the wisdom of your experience and the knowledge you have garnered through your life dictate.

When you will forgive yourself and the others for the things you believe have hurt you.

Nothing can happen without somehow willing it.

It is difficult to accept this, but my experience and the trials I went through have proven to me that this is the truth.

All the while I was carrying on my shoulders the burden of bitterness towards the people, I was unable to fly.

Every day my back was bending even lower. My back and my shoulders were in pain.

At the spots where my back should have to be strong in order to support the wings, I had wounds from the heavy burden.

Do you know why?

Because I was carrying over the pain from the past.

Because every moment I had negative thoughts for myself and for the others, I was adding weight to this burden.

There will come a time that you will be unable to get up from the ground.

You will be unable even to crawl. You will die crushed, though remaining alive, with eyes and ears open. With your heart beating and you mind screaming...

The daily death of spiritual life.

I know it well, because I have experienced all that.

81

Even today, when I have achieved many of my goals, I still learn and I still struggle to fly higher and higher.

I acknowledge, however, that I deserve it.

I have learned something of great importance.

Would you like to know what it is?

I will tell you.

But first, I am going to say something grandpa used to tell me.

"Define what Paradise means to you. This is what you have to remember daily. Every morning, as soon as you open your eyes, say: Today, I am experiencing Paradise. I choose and I undertake the responsibility of life in Paradise. Everything exists within us."

It took me many years and lots of travelling to understand this.

There are so many things that I want to tell you and this is why I am jumping from the one subject to the other.

I am an old woman now and, for me, death has become a loyal comrade. He can claim me at any time and lead me to the source of life.

However, as long as I live, I will be writing this letter.

Grandpa used to say that, from the moment of our birth, any moment is a probable moment of death.

This is why we should always be ready.

To be clean in our soul, to be free.

To have forgiven and to have asked forgiveness for whatever it is that it oppresses us even in our mind.

People say that, when you grow old, life is not worth living it anymore.

I am telling you that this is a lie.

Life is beautiful at any age, provided that you are not carrying any burdens and that you live in the light.

You are always learning.

What I have told you that I have learned, and it is important to me to learn about it, is: Choose what is worth it.

Learn to love what you are.

Every moment try to achieve the things you want.

Always make dreams and wish them to become reality.

Do not let your false self and the various problems lead you to the easy path of forgetfulness.

"You want to fly.

Where do want to go?

Into a future that is the same with the past?

You are flying from the present

and only into the present.

Your present is the view you have

about yourself and about life.

Do you want to see the world from above?

Stand up straight!

The more you realize your size,

the higher you will be flying.

We are huge!

We are infinite!"

The Mirror

I remember when, for the first time, grandpa taught me how to see the people's aura.

He took me by the hand and we went to the seashore.

It was summer, near the setting of the sun.

There, at the harbour, a loving couple, their heads touching, was enjoying the sunset.

A really beautiful picture of nature and people.

"Look at this couple," said grandpa. "Without focusing your eyes, travel in the image. When you are ready, tell me what you are seeing."

I was looking and looking. I could not see anything.

"Do not focus," said grandpa. "Look as if you are cross-eyed. Look where you think that there is nothing to see."

Then suddenly I saw something that looked like a milky sphere, surrounding them. It was pulsating, it had shape, and it seemed alive.

I could not explain it and I did not talk or move, afraid it would go away. The man got up and moved a bit farther.

I saw clearly one sphere separating from the other and now each person was surrounded by its own sphere.

I told grandpa, and he explained to me that this was what we call the 'aura' of people.

Grandpa taught me to trust in the things I was seeing and felt that, to me, they were true.

He taught me to follow the voice of my intuition. I learned to be able to see a world that was invisible to my eyes. I could communicate, and receive messages from somewhere, I knew not where. With grandpa's guidance, I had the sense that I was travelling in a different world, unknown, but wonderful.

Grandpa's favourite song had the lyrics: 'I did not travel to faraway places, the heart has travelled there' and that's enough for me.

We used to sing it together and his voice still resounds in my elderly ears.

His soul, he used to say, had 'travelled' to unknown, hidden worlds. He was seeing with the soul's eyes, he was feeling with his soul. It was as if he had travelled throughout the entire world.

It was as if he had loved all the women, all the men, all the children of this world, the entire creation of God.

He was indeed experiencing God.

His greatness.

Unfathomed able for the human mind, but not for the soul.

Because God and the soul are one.

"My soul thirsts to be searching, to explore," I would hear him say passionately. "I do not know what is that thing inside me that pushes me to do it, but I know that it is powerful and true. A great motive power. I am too humble to try to explain it. The only thing I know is that it is there, and I can feel it, I can experience it as the absolute truth."

How wonderful it is to be a human being and to seek to know what you are.

An entire unexplored, marvellous world!

"We are learning who we are from the others.
We are learning about the world through the others.
We are learning to live through the others.
We are learning to see through the others.
This is their truth.
Yet, is it ours as well?"

85

"One day, you will fly," grandpa would tell me. "One day you will see the world flying above it.

" But I want you to remember something at that hour: In order to see, to understand whether you are flying or not, do not look down look inside you."

Oh, dearest grandpa, how right you were.

There were moments in my life that I forgot your words and looked down.

I saw images, I heard words that unnerved me, that disappointed me. They brought me to irregular landings, that broke my wings and made me loath to fly once more.

You were well aware, grandpa, why you were telling me this! You knew what one would see, when one looked down.

But, grandpa, I also had to learn it. To experience it myself, in order to understand it.

It was not at all easy.

Many times, I tried to forget who I am.

But you were there to remind me.

You were inside me.

Your voice was resounding in the world of darkness, lighting it like a beacon.

That's how I made it, grandpa. Otherwise I would have remained forever hidden and frightened in my cave.

Darkness is much easier than light, when you are ignorant.

Light needs strength, courage, a will of steel.

It needs that you seek the truth inside yourself.

Disputing the truth of others and searching for your own. Not to take anyone's reality as un questionably your own.

The most difficult thing I have done on this Earth is to get to know myself, and to say: I am.

I love what I am.

I believe in my strength.

I am worth it!

From that time though, when I said it, everything changed in a magical way.

This was the magic you were telling me about.

Grandpa, you taught me to be a witch, without a magical wand.

"Everything in life happens in a magical way," you used to tell me grandpa. "You are solely responsible for the life you are creating for yourself. There are no excuses, evasions, half-truths. Only when you understand this, you will not blame others for what is happening to you. Then you will learn to deal with your world, and with what you are creating. Then you will be able to say I am and you will be. No one and nothing will be able to touch you.

" However, being responsible does not mean that you will not err at times.

" When you live, you also err.

" But, on the other hand, errors do not exist. Only experiences exist. When you will come to realize this, you should know that you only need very few feathers more in order to complete your wings.

" Be prepared to fly.

" Fly high!

> *"In order to understand*
> *what it means*
> *when we say*
> *that love liberates,*
> *you need to believe in yourself*
> *and in love.*
> *If you do not believe,*
> *then you are forging chains for you,*
> *your mate, your children."*

” This is your aim in life.

” Fly away, beyond the mountains, the seas, the plains, beyond the places you know.

” Fly into the un known.

” There, on the highest mountaintop you will find waiting for you...

” Who?

” You will see him as soon as you arrive.

” You will fly together to even higher mountaintops, to other unknown destinations.

” But, fly, fly!

” Do not let anything stop you.

” This is what you came for to the Earth. This what you live for.

” You did not come so that you would wallow in the mud. You did not come so that you will remain a handful of soil.

” You came in order to fashion wings and depart.

” In order to rise above the Earth.

” You came in order to fashion durable, strong wings, so that you may fly and find once more your road to the spring.

” My dearest, do not stay here.

” Fly, fly as far as you can.

” Fly high, as high as you can, every sing moment.

” You can, I am telling you. Do you want to?”

“I am afraid,” I would answer.

“You were born to be free.

” To fly through free skies.

” You are making your own skies.

” In unknown universes.

” The slaves of this world will never catch up with you anywhere.

” Do you know why?

” Because they have limits.

" They are frightened, just like the king in our fairy tale.

" The earth is parched. Their shapes and their life are emp ty. How can they understand you?

" How can they understand and accept someone who has the same shape, but also wings?

" They are going to call you a freak, an idiot.

" You will know why they are calling you that.

" You will know who you are and who are they.

" Then, their words will not rob you of feathers, but they will be adding to them.

" You will transform their words in a challenge, into power to rise higher than where you are.

" Higher, where you will be understanding even more things and the more you will be understanding the higher you will be flying.

" My dearest soul, put on your white cloak, let the wind play with your hair and you, free and strong, run with the tiger at your side!

" Extend your hand and receive the power, the blessing."

"But, Grandpa, how can I ignore the voices, the comments that tell me how useless I am?"

"It is no longer the others who are telling it to you; it is you who is repeating it to yourself."

"The others are telling it to me. They think that I am in ca- pable to make my dream come true. They criticize whatever I do or say. I am never right. I am always making some mistake or other. I would like to be as wonderful as the others are, so that they would accept me, so that they would want me to be in their world."

"I know who I am.

I trust what I am.

I can accomplish anything."

"Yourself, what do you believe about you?

"I am seeking through the others to see who I am."

"As long as you are going outside yourself, in order to find the truth about you, the only thing you are going to see is a lie. You are going to suffer, until you learn, until you are forced to look where you are bound to find yourself.

" Inside you.

" You are not what the others are seeing.

" At every moment, it is you who projects the image they are seeing, depending on what you believe you are."

"Do they believe about me what I believe, first of all, about myself?"

"Always! This is going to be happening until you change your self-image. But you have also to know what it is that you see in others, and it annoys you, and you won't accept it for yourself.

" Each one of us is a mirror of the others.

" The uglier the projections you are having, so many more are the rejected pieces of yourself. And this will go on happening, as long as you do not know who you really are."

"Do you mean to say that, actually, by putting the blame on some aspect of the others, I am blaming that aspect of myself, which I won't accept as having? And they see the same in me?"

"Exactly. Each one of us is a clear mirror of the other. Everything exists inside us. All people, all forms."

"How could this be?"

"I can be everyone, because I am everyone."

"Even the bad ones?"

"Even them."

"Then?"

"Then you understand. You do not need to exclude anyone from your love. Anyone can fly. Some later, some earlier. But

we all have come from the same source, and there we return."
The paths are different.

" The destination is the same.

" Forgiveness is the beginning of everything. Many times, in this life you will need to forgive yourself. No one is infallible. The basic principle, of course, is to respect the freedom and the free will of your fellow human being, and not to do something that you know it will harm him as a being. Neither by word nor by deed.

" Were you not to learn to understand and accept yourself, you will never be able to do it for another human being.

" Everyone needs love and forgiveness.

" If you do not understand this, you will remain stationary on your path.

" Who knows for how long.

" This is why you need to learn and to go forward.

" To go on to conquer impregnable castles, and reduce them to rubble.

" To keep your soul high and to conquer your world with love, respect, knowledge.

" Do go wherever you can, and extend your hand to whomever needs it.

" To have as your dream a sky filled with wings.

" Children flying in the timeless universe.

" This is why you have come in this world. Give me your hand!"

"When you have become used to the darkness,
you feel safer in there.
You prefer to underestimate the light
instead of finding out where you are
and then try to go towards it."

I would give it to him. A tiny hand in his huge, strong palm. I would lift my head and look at him.

He, too, was looking at me.

I could see tears streaming from his eyes.

He would take a bit of soil.

He would moisten it with his tears.

"Do you see?" he would ask. "Some of your feathers will be fashioned of clay and tears. At times tears of joy, at times of sorrow at other times of despair or of fear. You should remember all these moments. You should remember that eventually, if you wish it, they would become feathers for your wings. How much I wish I could see you when you will be ready to fly!"

Grandpa was not with me when his wish came true. I was late, by the earthly time. I am certain, however, that grandpa would have been very happy that finally I succeeded.

According to him, everything would happen at the right moment and time was following a different reckoning.

"What I am telling you," he used to say, "holds true for me. You will seek your own truth when you grow up.

" I do not want to persuade you that what I am saying is the sole truth. You will judge yourself which of all the things I have told you, you feel like keeping. Seek and find your own truth.

" All people are wise and they know what is best for them. So, listen, saying as little as you can, what the others have to tell you and let them, trusting their internal wisdom, to listen to their own self.

" But in order for them to do this, they need quietness; they need to hold onto a hand, which will remind them that they are not alone.

" Were you to sit quietly and listen to people, you will understand that our needs and our fears are the same.

" You will be surprised how identical they are.

" Then you will deeply love Man.

" You will understand him.

" It is magical, when you experience it…"

And grandpa started telling me a fairy tale.

"We have the

opportunity

in this life

to investigate,

to observe

and to heal ourselves.

Fear

is what keeps us stranded.

Life

is movement,

truth,

risk."

"The more we feel the need to blame others,
the uglier is the image we have for ourselves;
and the more hurt we are.
What's the use of blaming the mirror?"

An Arrogant Wise Man Learns His Lesson

Once upon a time, there lived a king, who was considering himself very wise. He believed that he, and he only, knew what was best for the others. He had a great dream: to make his wisdom known throughout the entire world and not only his, but also the wisdom of all the subjects of his kingdom.

So, he decided to turn into wise men, first of all, his councillors and his courtiers.

He started right away. He would gather them daily in the throne room and he would lecture them for hours on end.

He would dreamily shut his eyes while he was talking, happy that so many people were listening to him and because his dream had started becoming reality.

His words were indeed very beautiful and came from the depths of his soul. He believed that they were all listening to him, and so he increased the lecture hours, so that he would achieve his aim much faster.

But were the king to open his eyes, he would have seen this picture: of his people others were sleeping, others were scratching themselves, others were making small talk, others were picking lice off their clothes and hair...

The lectures of the king went on for days.

His courtiers and his councillors, having crushed all the lice they could find on either their head or on the head of their neighbours, having killed all the flies that were flying in the room, having swallowed all the mosquitoes that had fallen into the trap of their yawning mouths, decided that they could not take it any longer and resolved to revolt.

One evening, before the revolt, one of the king's councillors, and the only one who had been listening to the king's lectures, told him: this is what the others are going to do.

"Travel
to the place that
will never be explored
by anyone else
but you.
This 'place' is yourself.
The trip is long,
interesting,
into the unknown,
full of surprises
and unforeseen events.
This is why
Life is so fascinating."

The king and the councillor spent all night discussing why such a thing came to pass and what would be the best to do to solve the problem.

Finally, they decided. The king would go away for a few days, leaving as his regent the councillor. And so it was done.

When night fell, the king, dressed as a poor man, slipped away from the palace and took the road towards a snow covered, scraggy mountain. He wanted to find the wise old man who lived up there and to ask his advice.

Days and nights he travelled all alone, until he reached the old man' abode and knocked on the door.

"Welcome, young man," said the wise one, inviting him in.

"Most wise man," said the king, "I have come to ask your

advice. What to do so that all the people in my kingdom will become wise?"

"How do you know that you, yourself, are wise?"

The king started talking and he went on all night.

The old man did not utter a single word. He was just listening to him. But even had he wanted to say anything, he wouldn't have been able to get in a word edgeways, because the king did not stop even for a minute.

When eventually he finished, he asked the wise old man what did he have to say about all this.

Then the old man started talking the whole day long and there was no stopping him.

He prattled on and on and on...

The king, sleepless, tired, wondering at the incessant babbling, was thinking:

But what kind of a wise man is this one? Does he not understand when he should stop talking?

Most of what he is saying I know it well. But, by now, I can neither listen anymore nor understand any of the lot he has told me and continuous saying.

My head is boiling like the cook's cauldron the one in which she cooks for the entire court!

And, to give the devil his due, the cauldron was indeed huge.

In vain I walked all that way in order to talk to him, the king was thinking.

His babbling did not help me at all. I wasted my time.

He got up, disillusioned and angry, to go.

At the door, completely calm, the old man wished him a safe journey.

The king had turned to go, when he heard the wise man's loud voice saying:

"A wise man can also become a mirror!"

Surprised, he turned back to look, but the door had closed.

He was seething with anger in all the way.

What did the man mean?

That he, himself, was the same with that idiot who wanted to be called wise?

He refused to accept it.

At some point though, he started reviewing the old man's words.

What did the old man's behaviour was mirroring?

He kept going in circles around his kingdom, until he admitted that the wise man showed him what he, himself, was doing to others.

> *"The acknowledgement that we all have a purpose*
> *on this Earth, can change everything.*
> *Is our purpose for one to dominate the other?*
> *To appear better than the other?*
> *No.*
> *Our real purpose is spiritual."*

And from that moment on, the king changed.

He understood that each person knows what is best for one. He learned to hear more and speak less.

He also understood that the same wisdom we believe we have exists within all people and, if you wish to help them, you can do it by prompting them to understand it themselves.

To trust themselves.

The wisest advice is the one we give ourselves to us.

And so the king learned that we all have the same possibilities to acquire knowledge and we are all the same.

He had a long reign and he became even wiser and happier and so did we, and even more than him.

"And as Diogenes Laertius said," grandpa went on, "we have two ears and only one tongue, so that we hear more and talk less."

Many times, I had not paid any attention to the words I was saying to other people, believing that they would not be that important for them.

"You never know how a single word you have said, or an insignificant act, may affect someone," grandpa used to tell me.

As the words of other people had caused me pain, so I had also caused pain to others.

But I kept excusing myself, believing that they deserved it. In this way, however, I was becoming like them, saying subconsciously to myself: you deserve what you are being told, what is being done to you.

Then, how did I expect to achieve my goal?

Having such an image of one, how can you fly?

Wings cannot be fashioned in this way; they cannot carry such a weight.

"To fly you must have a light soul," grandpa would tell me. "It needs willpower, it needs strength, it needs resolve, it needs daily toil.

" You must say every day: I am Dionysia. I am deciding today that, no matter what happens, I am going to learn to fly and one day I will manage to fly. I can see very clearly myself flying.

" You have to consciously work on it every minute. You are in the present time. You are not lost either in the past or in the future. You are at the here and the now. You should say: I know and I can see clearly that I can do it! The future is altered every moment by the decisions of the present.

" What do I want done in order to be happy?

" It is a daily struggle.

" And it is a wonderful struggle, redeeming.

" Every day listen to your soul.

" Trust it, it knows how to guide you to your truth.

" How are you going to do this?

" You will be shutting your eyes and see what you really are inside you. Let your mind chatter. You know what you want to achieve. Let the Sirens talk away. Do not listen to them; otherwise you will never leave that place.

" See your luminous self. Ask it for enlightenment and give out healing light from the clear source of light that exists within you.

"What are you going to do today for your own good?
For the good of others?
Whom are you going to help in fashioning wings to fly?
You don't believe in it?
You don't feel like doing it for anyone?
Accepted.
This is how you feel at this moment.
But at least, for today,
do not try to break the wings of someone who is trying to fly."

" Ask whatever it is that is good for you it will be given to you with endless love and alacrity.

" You were made to be happy. You must remember this."

One day grandpa asked me to fashion a doll with my own hands. I did, using whatever materials I had.

She was so beautiful, I could not take my eyes from her.

"You love her so much, because she is your creation. Imagine, if we can love so much something we have created, how much more God loves us. Would it be possible for Him to want anything else for us, except our happiness?"

"But, Grandpa, in our world so many dreadful things are happening.

" What are all these?

" It looks as if there is no God.

" Were things as we are describing them, shouldn't He have put a stop to all these?

" What am I going to tell to the hungry children around the world? To those suffering torture?

'To those who have been molested?

" To those who have been sold as slaves?

" To those who age before they have even grown up?

" To those who have been taught to hate, to kill looking their victims straight in the eye?

" What shall I say to the parents whose children have been stolen, have been killed?

" What about the greed that kills you for your own good?"

"The answer is very, very difficult, and it is very good that you are asking the question," he said. "In your life, you must not ever be afraid. Whatever you may be told, ask questions no matter how hard you may think the answer is. Often the others get angry with us, simply because they do not have all the answers and they do not want to admit it. Do not ever pay any attention to it. Always ask questions and always have the courage to say what you want said. Let the other react in the way he deems right for himself.

" And now, I am going to tell you the answer I gave to this question, after a lot of thinking and observing.

" Because, I also, have wondered, many times, about all these things, and many times in my life I have questioned the existence of God. Naturally, in later years, you are going to give your own answers.

" Maybe for you God exists, but also He may be not. You are always free to give your own interpretation. Do not believe what others tell you. You will find, by yourself, what you do believe and why.

" Man has the inalienable right of choice. Every moment, it is he who selects his own road. Will he arrive to the source via the road of darkness, or through the light? Many times, if not in all of them, we need the experience of darkness, in order to consciously select the way of the light.

" It makes no sense that a God would compel us to do this or the other. As the parents do not control the choices their children make, so it is with God. Each one needs to experience one's own decisions.

"People need to be looked in the eye, to have their hand held
and to be asked how are they doing.
A piece of bread nourishes the body,
but it does not nourish the soul.
When you are giving that bread,
Touch those people's hands, look in their eyes.
So that they will see that you are doing it out of love
and not out of pity."

The greatest, selfless love is to give the best you can to your children, by your own example on how to live and behave, and then let them free to discover their own world.

" Children need acts, not only words. You cannot force any one to be what you think it is right that he should be. It makes no sense not to have conscious choices in our life, because otherwise the results would always be the same.

" This is why the choice of light by the individual is the greatest decision and it affects the entire humanity."

"A person alone can save the world?"

"Yes! Only one. Imagine the consciousness of each one. What do you think it adds up to?"

"The entire world."

"Kazantzakis said: 'Love responsibility; keep saying, I, all by myself, will save the world. If the world is gone, then I will be to blame.'

" You do not have to say anything to the suffering children. You can only act. If you wish, you will go to them and you will help them in any way you would be able to."

"Grandpa, the world is full of pain," I said.

Grandpa did not say anything for a while.

"I am not going to hide from you that what you are saying is true. But I will answer you with something Helen Keller said: 'Although the world is full of suffering, it is full also of the overcoming.'

" She was a deafmute, blind, American writer, who has been labelled the greatest 'miracle of willpower' of the Twentieth century. She learned to speak English, French, German, Greek and Latin. She was an eminent writer and a fighter for the good of humanity."

Grandpa used to say about the suffering children in the world: "Before you start feeling unhappy and sorry, ask yourself: What am I doing about it?

" What do I intent to do?

" If you under take to do something, even small, then you are contributing. Otherwise, stop grumbling, because it makes you seem as if you are expecting the others to do something for you.

" Helen Keller had said:

" 'I am only one, but still I am one. I cannot do everything, but still I can do something; and because I cannot do everything, I will not refuse to do something that I can do.'"

"Grandpa, are we, the common, humble, poor people powerless?"

"The world needs, my child, the small things that we, the common, humble people, can do. Because whatever we do, we do it from selfless love."

Mother Teresa used to say:

"Not all of us can do great things. But we can do small things with great love."

Mother Teresa was a nun who worked all her life for the relief of people in need.

She also said:

"In this world the hunger for love and respect is much more difficult to remove than the hunger for bread."

"Nothing
in this world
excuses
your feeling superior to someone else.
If you believe that you are superior to others,
then you are not appreciating
yourself
for what it is."

Spheres of Illusions.

At some point in my life, the time came to do what grandpa had told me. To give, with my, even so small contribution, as much as I could from my soul to those who had need of acts and not of words.

I travelled as volunteer to the African jungle.

It was a singular experience.

A different world.

Poor people, kind, decent, with a great civilization.

I was taught a lot from these people. And I experienced even more.

There were times when I would think that I would not be able to complete the programme I had undertaken, and I was crying from frustration.

It was an experience fraught with difficulties and dangers, but at the same time wonderful.

I did not give up.

I fought, and finally I succeeded.

I broke the known the barrier of my supposed limits.

I went much further than what I could understand until then.

I understood that the impossible does not exist.

It exists only until such time as we transform it into something possible.

Life functions in a magically beautiful way.

It is difficult to understand it, if we do not wish to experience it.

When you are seeking the truth, sooner or later you are going to find it in front of you.

You own quest leads you to it.

One day, on a deserted road, far away from the jungle village I was staying, two women were walking.

Myself, while I should have taken another, better road to reach my destination, I took that day the whimsical decision to take the other, the rougher, road which was the road these two women had taken.

They stopped me with shouts of joy and begged me to take them in my car as far as the hospital. The one of the two women was near giving birth.

There was not a single chance a car would be passing by that road neither then nor at any hour. It was a miracle that I had taken that road. Of course, I was more than happy to give them a ride to the hospital.

The woman, in order to thank me, did me the honour to ask me to be present at the birth of her child, which was about to emerge into the world.

Had I not followed my whim to take that road, the woman would have given birth, all alone but for her companion, in the middle of the jungle.

I accepted the honour.

It was one of the more powerful experiences in my life.

The woman had a natural, totally easy birth.

When the child started emerging, I felt the presence of God.

It was a powerful moment, between God and people.

There I dis covered that every human being that is being born is a miracle from God.

> *"What we say,*
> *what we think for us,*
> *for the world,*
> *whatever we do, affects us all.*
> *We are all responsible*
> *for our world."*

A pure, complete piece of God Himself.

I clearly saw the pure godly light of joy and love that was being born and was spreading to the entire room.

Inexplicable.

Inconceivable, how did we come to believe that some human beings are different because to their colour?

Does the colour of our skin makes us superior or inferior? The function of skin colour is the protection of the human skin.

So, how come that the colour and the nationality became reasons for discrimination?

Yes! We the common people, humble, poor, insignificant, we can change the world.

How?

For me the answer is something Mahatma Gandhi, the great Indian leader said:

"A man is the sum of his actions, of what he had done, of what he can do. Nothing else."

Buddha said:

"Thousands of candles can be lit from a single candle, and the life of the candle will not be shortened. Happiness never de creases by being shared."

We all are that small, single candle of Buddha.

Love does not lessen by being given to others.

The light we are made of does not diminish.

The kind word, the caress, the warm hug, the small aid to someone in need does not deprive us of anything. On the contrary, they grow inside us, illuminating us even more.

Why should we be stingy with something that has been freely given to us?

Something we are made of and which is infinite and eternal?

Grandpa used to tell me: "Do you think that, when we depart this world, we are going to take with us anything of all these all the material things we need in this life in order to live it?

" Even if all the people in the world are working for our benefit and even if all the wealth on this Earth belongs to us, what are we going to be able to take with us?

" We will barely fit in the crate the undertaker will put us in. It's so tight, our hands cannot be laid on our sides.

" Eh, well, if you can afford a larger casket, a deluxe one, perhaps it will be more comfortable you will be able to stretch your arms, man!

" But, unfortunately, it cannot hold either our great mansion or our fabulous car, or the moneyboxes we have accumulated, or anything else.

" So? What has real value on this Earth?

" For me only one word is really valuable.

" A word that you need to think of on your deathbed.

" Which word describes the life you have lived?

" Did I kill my brother for one measure of land?

" Did I kill for power?

" For money?

" For glory?

" Did I steel?

"Trust yourself.
Trust the people.
Even if they disappoint you,
the world won't come to an end.
You are not responsible
for the other people's choices.
Only for your own."

" Did I wrong people?

" Who am I?

" Did I give love?

" Did I give something of what I had in my soul?

" Did I do good deeds wherever and whenever I could?

" What have I learned?

" Is what I know the only truth?

" The earlier you will learn that word, so much better for you. Then you will know where you were and where you have arrived.

" It does not matter in the least if you have crossed the darkness in order to reach the light.

" It matters where do you find yourself right now.

" Were you to stop at the problems and at all these that happen around you, were you to keep contemplating the mistakes of the past, you will be turned into a pillar of salt like Lot's wife. If you can see the light, go towards it, even if no one else can see it.

" You will need to struggle. The difficulties are for the strong ones and for those who want to become even stronger."

Do you want to know what I have understood, after all these years I have lived on this Earth?

Everything is a well-staged illusion.

Each one of us lives inside a virtual sphere.

He is all alone, but he is creating his world in accordance with what he has seen and heard as a child.

In growing up, he changes the shape of his illusions, but the script remains the same.

Each one, in his little sphere, creates a huge world and does with it as he wishes.

A lot of work, indeed!

Things happen in this earthly dimension that keep us alone and each one secluded in his virtual sphere.

As long as we are weaving, thought by thought, the illusions of our world, we will never get out from it.

Only with the magical word, We, ourselves can shatter the sphere.

Only when we will stop being afraid of our self, but also of the others.

And of course, each one of us carries inside his sphere fears, insecurities, convictions that determine specific behaviours.

All these, and many more, are hooks.

Each hook has ropes that hold us securely tied into the sphere of illusions.

How to free yourself from all these?

Difficult?

Very.

Impossible?

No.

The important thing is that it is not impossible.

Do you know why?

Because it not the truth we are made of.

It is a huge lie, with which they have prepared us to face a false world.

"Check out what kind of a world
you are creating within your sphere.
Do you like what you see?
If yes, go on as before.
If no, do something about it.
Your life is the things you believe in.
Solutions are always available.
Ask and you will be given."

It is us who believe it as the only and undisputed truth that we know and that exists.

Yet, is it?

Each one has the right to give one's own answer in this life. What I have to say, and also my grandpa used to say, is: "Search before you answer."

One by one, each person who reaches self-actualization, who becomes one's real self, stops playing the roles imposed on him and which he has learned to play.

It is then that spheres of illusion will stop being created. When we will no longer be writing scripts, when we will no longer pretend, we are actors.

When there will exist only the clear, true, free self of each of us.

Difficult?

Yes!

Impossible?

No!

"Will it take many years, Grandpa, for this to happen," I would ask him.

"Time does not exist. Only within the sphere there is the sense of time."

"What happens within the sphere of each one of us?" "Within our sphere we produce a great quantity of energy. " We work incessantly for that. Day and night, night and day."

"What tools are we using?"

"Our thoughts. " These thoughts produce either positive or negative energy. These energies feed corresponding sources."

"Grandpa, what is happening right now on the Earth?" "Right now on the Earth, my child, if we observe what is going on, we can say that the sphere of each one, his world, functions with negative thoughts and produces more negative than positive energy.

" This is why we are seeing all these horrors happening around us. War, hunger, cruelty, murders and other awful things, that are beyond my imagination."

"Do you mean to say that if we change the way we are thinking, the reality of the whole world will change?"

"Yes, it can change."

"But if we continue having negative thoughts?"

"Then the things we will be seeing happening around us will become increasingly negative."

"Grandpa, I am afraid."

"No! There's nothing to be afraid of when you know the truth. Only then you know what you need to do. While you are living in deceit, in falsehood, you do not.

" Do you know the etymology of the word 'aléthia' ('truth' in Greek)?"

"No."

"Now listen: the word is composed from the negative pre fix 'a' and the word 'léthe', meaning 'oblivion'.

So 'aléthia' is: what I am not forgetting.

" In another explanation the negative prefix 'a' is combined with the word 'létho', meaning 'to escape'.

" So, 'aléthia' is: what does not escape me.

"Today do not forget to see the truth,
the love of the people around you.
See it as a bright light.
You, too, should contribute to its propagation.
Get out of the cave's darkness.
Only our combined effort can make the difference."

" The wisdom of our ancestors is contained in a tiny word. This is the Greek language. Study it and you will understand. As you will understand why some powerful people want to hold us back from learning it."

"Oh, Grandpa, you do explain everything in a great way! I promise you I will study the Greek language."

"Now, listen to this, so that you may understand something more about our world, according to the 'theory of ideas' as propagated by Plato.

" Plato, this great Greek philosopher, wishing to point out how difficult it is to comprehend truth and what we experience as truth, recounted the following allegorical myth:

" 'Men seem to be chained hands, feet, neck, in a cave from which they cannot get out and they are chained in such a way that they are unable turn their head. Behind them, a fire is burning. In front of the fire, on a ramp, various things are passing by, men, animals and other stuff. The only thing men see from all this parade that goes on behind their back are its shadows, as they are cast on cave wall in front of them. All things and images are distorted. They have no relation to reality. Yet, men trusting the image their constricted vision is giving them, an image they are familiar with and which they accept believe, beyond any doubt, that the distorted shadows are the only truth.

" And even if someone would manage to get out into the light, the brightness of the sun would blind him if he is not open minded, and so he would go back to what he knows as being true. Back to the darkness of the cave, back to slavery, to deceit. In there he feels more secure. If, on the contrary, the light does not blind him, he is able to see. Consequently, when he would go back and tell his comrades what he has seen, he may very well be faced with hate, for deceiving them with his lies. They could even kill him, were they to think that he is trying to blind them.'"

"But then, Grandpa, wouldn't it be better for one to keep quiet?"

"Well, Plato used to say that even if such a danger exists, it should not stop you from telling your comrades the truth."

"Do our senses lie to us?"

"Our senses create hallucinations and illusions, derived from the conviction that we are separate from one another, from our thirst for power, for riches, and for a score of other deceitful shadows. Being chained, the only thing we can see is that huge deception."

"How can we break the chains?"

"Plato maintains by self-awareness. I agree with him."

"Do we live in a deception or in a lie?"

"To me deception is being in Plato's cave, since we do not know the truth.

" Only whoever comes into the light becomes aware of it.

" On the other hand, we live in a lie when we know the truth, but we are consciously creating for some reason of our own a new reality."

"Taking the decision
to be healed
is by itself a kind of healing.
After that whatever we need
will appear in our way."

Healing Light

There were difficult moments in my life, and certainly they were not few.

At the beginning I certainly did not want to accept the way I was feeling.

I was refusing to change it.

Covering my eyes with my hands, I was abandoning myself to deadlocked thinking.

Then I would remember grandpa's virtual spheres.

What kind of energy am I producing right now?

I would observe my thoughts.

I had to admit they were negative.

Therefore, I was feeding the continuation of my misery, of the deadlock, of the pessimism, of the compromise.

Not only for me, but for others, too. Because, although we do not understand it, when we are negative or positive towards our self, we are influencing the actions and the life of other people around us.

Do I want to continue like this forever?

If yes, then I am doing fine. I'll go on.

If not... Then I have a responsibility.

I would lift up my head and start declaiming: I am Dionysia. I can see quite clearly the − −, whatever it was that each time I wanted done, so that I would feel happy.

Because yes, happiness does exist. As long as you are not lukewarm with life and with the things you want to experience. Life is tension!

Life is passion!

Many times I have drawn back, because I was afraid of making a mistake.

And what if I would do something that could condemn me to an unhappy life?

The probability of a mistake was, for me, a really serious reason for not living as I wanted to live.

If because of that move I would make, the others would think badly of me?

If they would reject me? How could I bear it?

So I remained stationary.

In this way I avoided the danger of making a mistake.

I was not in danger from a possible failure.

I avoided criticism.

But when I spoke to grandpa about my fears, he answered me with a fairy tale.

"The beauty that lasts through time
lies inside us.
The more we grow the more it reflects on our face
how we have lived our life.
How we were thinking.
How we were treating ourselves and the others."

"Say a word that will aid someone in his life.
Do something for the one who needs you.
You are lighting a flame in someone's life.
Perhaps tomorrow
a strong wind may put out your flame
and you will need once more
the light of your own flame
from the one that you had once given it.
Transmit the good."

The Cave of Healing

Once upon a time, there was a king.

He was just and he was governing his kingdom in the best possible way. But he was daily carrying a sadness deep inside him that did not let him be happy and enjoy his life. He was afraid of taking the wrong decisions and he was afraid of old age. His sorrow was going on and every day it was getting worse. He could no longer take any decision, even about himself. Everything seemed to him insurmountable. Life had no longer any meaning for him.

His councillors realized that something should be done. So they spoke to him about the mountain where the cave of healing was to be found.

He agreed to go there. It was a very difficult trip. Many times he thought of going back, but he always went on. Indeed, after a great effort and many struggles, he arrived at the cave.

He recognized it, because two beautiful eagles guarded it. "No one goes in, unless he gives the right answer," they told him.

"What is the question?"

"There is no question," answered the eagles.

"Then, what answer should I give?"

"You will have to find out, if you want to go in," they said.

The king was thinking, trembling in agony. He had to be unerring. He was a king. He sat there, outside the cave, for days. He would prefer to leave than give the wrong answer.

One day, as he was sitting there, desperate and tired, ready to give up and take the road back home, he saw a young man, poorly dressed, coming towards the cave. His eyes shone with a strange light.

He greeted politely the king and asked him whether he had been healed.

The king said that he still had not managed to get in.

"You are here before me," said the young man. "If I give the right answer, I will let you go in my place."

"Do not fear anything or anyone.
The stronger,
the wiser man in the world
lives inside you.
He is always there for you."

"But if you afterwards will not been able to answer the question, they will give you, you will not be able to get healed," said the king to the young man.

"Yet, for the time being, I'm going to do what I think is right. I will take the risk of my decision," answered the young man.

So the young man appeared before the eagles and they asked him the same question.

"Every answer is right, if it leads to healing," said the young man.

The eagles gave way.

The young man offered his turn to the king, as he had promised.

The king went in. He was expecting to see, to hear something. All was darkness and silence.

He stood there for hours. Nothing.

He was wrong, in the end, for taking the young man's place.

He did not deserve to be healed.

He dropped to the floor, heavy with sorrow.

He would want very much to see this thing that felt so heavy on him and did not let him enjoy his life.

He joined his hands at his breast and said: "Light of healing, I want to be healed!"

Then, from the depths of the cave, he saw a light coming towards him.

When it came near, he saw two joined palms and between them was flowing the brightest, strongest, most serene light he had ever seen.

The hands took his own between them, and a sweet calm ness spread inside him.

He felt rather than heard the following words:

"Forgive yourself for whatever error you may be ascribing to it. You always did the right thing, in accordance with the knowledge you had at that particular moment.

" Today, you are thinking that you could have decided differently.

" But today, your thinking is different. Every minute we go on developing, we go on learning, we do not remain stationary. You cannot condemn yourself for errors you believe to have committed or to be constantly in fear of the error you may commit.

" Nothing happens by chance. There are no errors, just experiences.

" You say: I made a mistake.

" All right, let us accept that you did.

" What are you going to do now about it?

" Are you going to get sick?

" Are you going to die?

" Are you going to condemn yourself to a life of sorrow and to a living death?

" What do you expect to achieve by this?

" You are simply missing the opportunity to learn, to live. Go on, go beyond the error. Perhaps, next time you will not repeat it.

" Every moment it is you who chooses how to see things.

" The fear of error will always keep you outside life. To live means to make mistakes.

" Not making mistakes, means I am not living.

"Every day we may choose:
Do we want to grow older and sillier,
hanging on he departed beauty of the flesh,
or lighter and more wise?"

" Every moment we are doing the best we can for ourselves and for the others. This is what we are at that moment. We cannot know if tomorrow we may come up with a better solution. The only thing I know is the 'now'.

" This is what I am in the now, and I cannot think beyond that.

" Live and do the best you can at every moment. The passing of the years, you are so afraid of, will change your face. It will not change your essence.

" But you will have to choose what you are going to do every day of your life.

" Will you be learning to become even brighter or you will be letting yourself to be sucked away by the darkness?

" Each particular age is holding different lessons. Greater knowledge.

Until the day of our death, we are experiencing, we are learning.

" Why stop?

" Because you have wrinkles?

" If you are going to carry on with this fear, you will not experience anything. You will always be angry and tired. Life will be passing in front of you, and you will be feeling feeble.

" A living dead."

The king was relieved of his burden. He came out of the cave feeling light as a feather.

"I will wait for you to come out," he said to the young man and sat down on a rock to wait, a happy man.

When the young man presented himself to the two eagles, they asked him:

"Which is the scraggiest, the most beautiful mountain in the world, which has no peak and for which you need a lifetime to climb it?"

"The mountain of my soul," he answered.

The eagles stood aside.

When the young man got out, the king was waiting for him. The light in the young man's eyes was shining even brighter. He was entirely made of light.

The king offered him the position of crown councillor. "When you believe that everyday life brings you the best, when your thoughts are beautiful, when you do good to yourself and to the world, then, finally, the miracle happens. Things you have not even imagined, come your way," said the young man and gladly accepted the king's offer.

And as the years were going by, the king and his councillor were becoming wiser and happier and even more did we.

"At times life resembles a vast morass
where the more you resist the deeper you sink,
and at others it becomes a wonderful golden beach,
where you enjoy the warmth
of a bright sun under a blue sky.
If you find yourself in the morass,
calm yourself.
The time of the beach will come.
It always does."

"The light of forgiveness," said grandpa, "is the light we need more than anything in this world. Many ropes get cut, many hooks get broken in the sphere.

" Forgive yourself now, whatever it may be what you are blaming him for."

"Grandpa, if I forgive, will the others do the same for me?"

"I will answer you with a line by Kazantzakis: 'I am not afraid of God; He understands and He forgives. I am afraid of the people. They neither understand nor forgive.'

Whom do you think you should, first of all, understand and forgive?" grandpa asked me.

"Myself," I answered.

"I agree with you. If you sit quietly and listen to people, you will realize that we all fear the same things. We have the same desires, the same common experiences, insecurities, dreams. We all have the same need for love and acceptance. You have to respect your fellow human being, understand him, look deeply into his eyes with love.

" Jesus Christ said: 'Thou shalt love thy neighbour as thyself.'

" I wonder. Do we love our self?

" Do we forgive it that, may be, it is not as intelligent as we would wish, as funny, as good, as handsome, as talkative, as... as... so that we may love it?

" You will see that, by helping someone get healed, you are also healing yourself.

" That's how much we are connected to each other.

" Harming someone, means that I am also harming myself.

" Hurting someone, I am also hurting myself."

"Grandpa, what is the etymology of the Greek word for 'forgiveness'?"

"The Greek word is 'syghoresis'. From the prefix 'syn', meaning 'plus' and the verb 'horo', meaning 'space', the combination denoting 'I give space'. That is to say, I give some space to the other to sit next to me and talk to me. I am letting him tell me his own truth.

" This understanding takes me out of my private hell. Personally, my idea of hell is to be stuck on something.

" I can be stuck on thinking about someone, in my anger, and the more I resist the deeper I am sinking.

" I forgive.

" And so I liberate him and I liberate myself."

My soul would open like a flower and receive the drops of dew in the guise of grandpa's words.

" Every time I am thinking about it, I have the same sensation. My soul becoming tender and then blooming into a beautiful flower, thirsting for those dewdrops that would give it clarity and life.

Were it once in a while to tell grandpa that someone had annoyed me with his words or deeds, he would ask me to de scribe to him exactly what had happened.

If he would judge that it had been my fault, we would discuss it and I would understand. Then I would go to the person in question and apologize. He was teaching me not to carry inside me the burden of injustice and bitterness.

Were he to judge that it had not been my fault, he would tell me one of Socrates' maxims:

"If a donkey kicks you, it makes no sense for you to kick it back."

Grandpa used to say that laughter is one of the most beautiful things in life.

To laugh, to be happy, to let your soul open to the beautiful and the good.

To that end he would tell me a funny story most of which was in fact true.

"Today find a reason to laugh,
to smile.
Smile to a butterfly,
to a flower,
to the sun,
to the clouds,
to the rain.
Laugh with the laughter of a child.
Smile to yourself.
There is always beauty around us.
We see it only when we want to."

The Greedy Priest

Once upon a time, there was a fat priest, who was living with his spouse in a small town.

He wanted to eat all the time.

"Stop eating for a bit, my good man," his wife would tell him. "Your belly has become so huge that it can hold an entire calf!"

But he would burp and say:

"Food is the God's blessing."

One day he was invited to officiate at a saint's feast day at a mountain village. He went with great pleasure, looking forward to the festivities that would follow.

The moment the Holy Mass ended, he fell to eating. He was eating anything he could lay his hands on.

And as he had his hands full with nuts and honey sweets, pancakes, spicy slices of cake and what not, a woman offered him an appetizing piece of roast meat.

"But can't you see, my good woman," he shouted eagerly, "that my hands are full? Do put it straight into my mouth."

The woman did so and screamed in terror! The priest nearly ate her hand.

In the evening the villagers invited the priest to spend the night at the squire's house.

They set the table for supper boiled chicken and chicken rice soup with egg and lemon sauce.

"My favourite," the priest managed to utter, and fell to the dish. Before the others around the table had even brought the first spoonful to their mouth, he had cleaned his plate and he was chasing the last grain of rice that kept escaping him.

"Do you want a second helping, Reverent?" they asked him. "Even God wants another one."

This one had the same fate. But this time the priest also started licking the plate.

"Do you want some more, Reverent?" they asked him once more.

"Eh! Let's complete the Holy Trinity..."

He also devoured the entire boiled hen, as well as whatever else was on the table.

His hosts were afraid he might eat them too!

They put him in their son's room to sleep, because he said he preferred to sleep upstairs.

They gave him a basin full of water and a towel, so that he may wash his face in the morning, and a pitcher full of water, in case he would feel thirsty during the night.

The priest went to bed and slept like log.

After a while loud thunders were shaking the entire house. "Hey, wife, what's happening in high summer?" said the squire, lifting his head from the pillow. "Is there a thunderstorm?"

"What thunderstorm, you silly? It is the priest who is farting," said his wife.

"Oh! Our Godawful luck! He will bring our house down."

In the night the priest got thirsty. He drank the entire pitcher, plus the water in the basin, which had been destined for his ablutions. He went back to bed, slept like a log.

He saw a dream.

'With the full moon as his lamp,

The young man is roasting a lamb...'

He awoke up, hungering for food.

But as he was cudgelling his brains where to find something to eat, he was taken with a great sudden colic.

Where to go?

What to do?

He took the basin and started crapping and crapping and he could not stop.

He wiped his arse with the towel they had given him to wipe his face.

He took the basin and emptied the shit out of the window.

What to do with the towel he had so dirtied?

He threw out that too.

However, every night, the young girl from the house across the street used to go to the room of her beloved the family's son climbing up a ladder she would lean on the wall under the window.

The thing is, she had no idea that tonight the room had a different tenant.

She was climbing the ladder, looking up with yearning for her beloved. She was in a hurry...

Well, everything fell on her head!

"What on earth is this? Shit!!! By the bucketful..." She got the dirty towel on top of everything else.

She climbed down as best she could.

She barely escaped falling and breaking her neck. She ran back to her home.

After a while, a thief went by, hugging the wall.

He stepped on the shit. It filled his shoes. He couldn't care less.

He went to the barn. He stole a lamb.

The theft was discovered the next morning. The squire and his farm hands followed the trail. They came under the priest's window. They saw the ladder.

"You ate the lamb!"

"I did not!"

They were arguing for hours.

Said the priest:

"I swear to you. I did not eat the lamb. I was farting too much."

They believed him. Anyway, they had heard him all night long.

At that moment a hunter came running. He had caught the thief hiding in the forest, with the lamb. They put the thief in gaol. They celebrated the event with much food and much dancing. And, of course, the priest ate more than all the rest combined.

They lived well and we lived even better.

> *"Today,*
> *do not hear only about the ugly,*
> *bad things that happen in the world.*
> *Fear,*
> *pessimism,*
> *resignation,*
> *are the greatest forms of control.*
> *Search and find the good things that are happening.*
> *Perhaps they are many more than you imagine."*

The Flame of the Good

I remember one day, when, disappointed by myself and by people, I said to grandpa:

"In the end I believe that people do not deserve my love.

They are very cruel, selfish, meanspirited; they care only about themselves.

" They sacrifice people, lives, at the altar of wealth.

" They want to sweep away anything that is different. Anything that does not agree with what they believe in.

" They enjoy hurting others.

" They kill, they injure, they molest, they exploit consciences and people so that they may become rich; they hurt others so that they may feel powerful.

" How come that we deserve that higher perception, you were telling me about, of being called hu man beings?

" In what kind of a world you expect me live?

" How can I be happy among all these?

" I did not ask to come into such a world, as the one you have made."

"Did you get to know the entire mankind, and so formed this opinion?" asked grandpa.

"Eh... no!" I answered, taken aback by his question.

"I will answer you with something Mahatma Gandhi once said: 'You must not lose faith in humanity. Humanity is like the ocean; if a few drops of the ocean are dirty, the ocean does not become dirty.'

" As long as they are people who keep the flame burning, do not be afraid of anything.

" Even better it would be for you to become one those people.

" Yourself to change the world.

” You are given a chance in this lifetime.

” Remember Kazantzakis, who said: 'poor man, you can move mountains'.

” Don't learn about it at the hour of your death. Acquire this knowledge much earlier.

” Do what Socrates had urged us to do: 'Use your time to improve yourself. Learn by reading the writings of other people, so that you will acquire easily what they have worked hard in or der to produce it.'

” We have been given invaluable knowledge and wisdom.

” All exist inside us.

” Our ancestors did climb their own mountains. They have left us a great wealth of experiences. You, too, should also take advantage of them.

” The quicker the soul, the higher the mountain.

” The more difficult the climb.

” The higher you go, the obstacles are more, and bigger, the enemies more numerous.

” Kazantzakis said: 'Do not deign to ask: Shall we win? Shall we lose? Fight!'

” Fight for yourself, for humanity.

” You + Man + Humanity = One.

” Keep the flame burning.

” You can do it.

” You can do it! Do it.

” See the flame.

” Envision your act.

” Become one of the fairies of the lamp," said grandpa.

"Now let me tell you a fairy tale ..."

"If you are one of those who want to keep the flame burning,

what are you going to do about it today?

If you believe

that you cannot do something yourself,

then observe the world around you diligently

and with knowledge.

You are going to see many things you are daily passing by,

thinking that they are of no importance.

Just observe."

.

The Fairies of the Lamp

Once upon a time there were seven fairies.

They lived in a beautiful house, fashioned of magical myrtle boughs.

They wanted the light of good to shine all over the world.

They had an oil lamp, the flame of which should never go out. They were guarding it all day long and all night long.

In the forest, across from their place, seven wicked witches lived in a big castle.

They wanted the oil lamp to go out and evil to get its claws on the world.

They were constantly thinking how to bring this about.

One day, the first one says:

"I will go!"

She shifts her shape to a sweet old woman.

She goes to the forest of the fairies and say: "I've brought you a little oil for your good little lamp."

The fairy lifts the bottle to the light. The oil is black.

"We do not put this kind of oil in this little lamp," she says. The witch leaves, frustrated.

The second witch says:

"I will go."

She goes. She shifts her shape to a little mouse.

She gets inside.

The fairy sees it, she becomes a cat and she eats it.

The others were waiting for her to come back. Nothing.

The third says: "I will go."

She goes. She shifts her shape to a feather. She gets inside. The fairy sees it; she becomes a gust of wind.

She blows and the feather flies over the flame. It is turned into ashes.

Hopelessly the other witches are waiting.

"I will go," says the fourth. "I will succeed."

She goes. She shifts her shape to a black cloud. She gets inside.

The fairy becomes sun. She dissolves the cloud.

The other witches see that neither this one is coming back.

"I will go," says the fifth.

She goes. She shifts her shape to rain. She cannot get through. She becomes more and more violent. She succeeds.

All the fairies run and make a circle around the lamp and say:

'This poor lamp of ours
lights all the world all hours.
It tames all wickedness repugnant.
The good will always be triumphant!'

The rain falls into the lamp. Evaporates with a bang.

So great is the bang that the sound reaches the witches' castle.

The first and the seventh witch have been left alone.

They say: "Now we will go together, to chase the good away."

They go. They shift their shape to king and queen. They turn the stones into soldiers and the pieces of wood into swords.

They cry: "Open your door right now, gifts to receive with our bow!"

The fairies answer: "None is entering our halls, matters not what gifts he hauls. Only a soul pure to the core can open this here door."

The wicked witches order the soldiers:

"Kill them all!"

With horrible shouts, the soldiers draw their sword and attack.

Then the entire forest resounds with the loud voices of the fairies, declaiming these magical words:

'Oh, breath so great of the truth,

You who in the tales lives forsooth,

Blow upon the lamp, the flame to flare up high

to disenchant all those creeps who dare go by!'

And indeed, so it happened.

A huge flame shoot up from the lamp and all the spells of the wicked witches came to nothing.

Ever since, the flame of the humble lamp is burning unimpeded.

No one ever managed to take it from the fairies, and all those who tell fairy tale s keep the flame eternally burning in their heart. They lived well forever after, and we lived even better.

> *"We are made of light.*
>
> *This is why it is difficult for us*
>
> *to experience the darkness.*
>
> *But this is also a rite of passage.*
>
> *An experience."*

As soon as he finished the fairy tale, grandpa asked me:
"Do you think it is easy to keep the flame burning? I tell you it isn't. Many will want to put it out and many will try it.

" But, by then, you will have learned to fly. You will have been wondering and you would have understood why you are here.

" A large feather in your wings will be when you learn that you do not need to wait for the others to appreciate what you are or what you do.

" Always do what your soul wishes for.

" Because this is what you are. You know this, beyond any doubt. You are not better than anyone else. You are not worse than anyone else. You are you. Unique, as each one of us is." You are the one who knows who you are.

" Osho has said: 'The real man remains ordinary, completely ordinary. No one knows who he is, no one knows of the treasure he is carrying inside him. He never advertises the person, he never tries to put himself forward. But we, why do we advertise ourselves? Because of our ego. You are not satisfied with yourself. You are satisfied only when the others appreciate you.'"

"Grandpa, who was Osho?"

"Osho was an Hindu mystic, a great philosopher and spiritual teacher of international renown."

"His words are beautiful, Grandpa."

"How do you expect to be appreciated by someone who does not know and appreciate first of all himself?" grandpa would ask me.

"In order to appreciate another human being, you need first of all to have become acquainted with and to have ap appreciated yourself.

" So do not rely on anyone's opinion when you want to go forward.

" Each of us is able to see things, depending on the height of the mountain where he has found himself at each particular moment.

" Your duty is to be fashioning your wings, so that you can fly. Only you are in a position to know who you are."

"Having a good opinion of myself, does it mean I am an egoist?"

"It does not if you do not lower someone else so that you may appear superior. Many times, because we feel small and in significant, we are trying to diminish the others in our eyes, so that we may feel taller. We need, of course, to be also open to criticism. Perhaps in it there is a message for us, a lesson that will help us develop and, maybe, we see in our self-something, which we have refused to admit.

" Yet, this should not dishearten you and make you say: No, I am not good enough to succeed.

" Listen, judge, take the best that's offered and become stronger, so that you will acquire more power and will fly even higher.

"We judge and we are judged daily
for our words and our deeds.
Criticism aids one towards one's development.
But when it's purpose is to wound,
to lower one's self-esteem,
then it may destroy lives,
especially those of the children.
Because it is we who are teaching them about the world,
about life, about happiness, about despair."

" There will be day when you will feel like mud and others when you will feel that you are an eagle.

" Everything is fine. Everything has a reason for happening.

" Do not let anything and anyone stop you.

" Nothing remains the same.

" Everything can change from one moment to the next.

" It is enough that you lift up you head and look at the light.

" Take a run and fly!

" Today. Now.

" Do not wait.

" Miracles can happen, suffices that you want them to happen. This is my advice," said grandpa.

When I had written my first book, I met, through some acquaintances of mine, a famous writer. I wanted him to aid me with the experience he had in publishing.

I went to meet him

He took my manuscript in his hands, read a random page and told me: "This book has no market value. People do not buy this kind of books. Better write a love story, or go get married and have a few children. In this way you will realize your aim and you will repay your debt to society. The people do not understand this kind of trite philosophizing. No one bothers with this stuff. Give them love and sex fantasies, if you wish to make money."

I thanked him for his time and left with my tail between my legs.

I was once more in danger of giving it all up.

This was my initial thought. The man's arguments were quite persuasive with regards to the book's failure and my low-quality writing.

Certainly, this was not the first time that neither my book nor its subject had met with disapproval. But, by listening to criticism, I had become stronger.

In my mind I was hearing ever more clearly the words of Kazantzakis, as my grandpa was reading them:

"When we are passionately believing in something that does not exist, eventually we create it. What has not happened is what we did not desire enough."

Today, at my age, and with the experience I have accrued, I can assure you that this is absolutely true.

The book that writer (and others) read and rejected, as well as my ability to write, travelled through the entire world and was translated into several languages.

Yet, through all this, what made me fly even higher were the people who were saying to me that my book spoke to their soul and that, because of it, they have fashioned even a small feather for their wings.

"Today
I choose to live with love and to forgive.
Tomorrow
it may be too late for all.
What will accompany me when I shall leave?
I came alone.
I will leave alone.
What shall I take with me so that I will feel secure?
Money?
Power?
Fame?
Houses,
enterprises, – or –?
Let each one give one's own answer."

What more would I wish for?

Jesus Christ said: "Even if you help one soul by word or deed in this life, it is enough; it is a lot."

But if fame and recognition is you your only goal, your motive for anything you are doing, this is so much like a hot air balloon.

These things are very nice when they occur, but they are not an end in themselves.

I wanted strong wings, real wings; wings with which to fly and communicate not only with the people's souls but also with my own.

These books were my healing process. Before to anyone else, I was talking to me.

And so I have managed, through all these experiences, to find myself and to understand my power.

I have made my holiest dream reality.

I have managed to make my goal my life.

I have felt love in all its glory.

I am happy for this.

My soul feels as if sitting on downy clouds and travelling around the world approaching and touching anyone who is holding in his hands one of my books.

Because this feat is a creation to which we have all contributed.

Success did not come because I imparted some secret or other, or something that it is not known to everyone.

The success of one person is the success of all.

It is the justification of one person's struggle; of the strength that lies inside us and urges us to fight, to turn into reality our dreams, our soul's desires.

Had they not been people who love, wonderful souls to the existence of which, first grandpa and then myself believed in no one would have understood my first book, and it would not have had any success.

In one of my endeavours to get it published, I met a publisher who, although he did not undertake its publication, told me:

"You merit to be published, you are a talented writer. Do not give up."

I believed him, because he was a true human being, whom I never forgot, and his words gave me courage all these years when I was struggling not to give up.

A few words kept a person's dream alive.

When one contemplates it, it seems almost holy.

Real greatness...

Hadn't there been selfless people in this world, who gave their aid with the sole purpose of seeing another person's dream come true, this dream of mine would never have become reality.

God on the one hand, myself on the other and all of us together, finally we did it!

I believed in myself, in the beauty of the human being, in our unlimited potential.

I believed in the God inside me the God who has no name, nor wealth, or power, the God who does not kill in order to make people believe in Him.

But He is freedom and the pure light of love.

I have managed to break some of the chains holding my neck, so that I could turn, even a little, my head to see behind me the fire that burns and creates the shadows I believed they were the sole reality.

Many times I thought I was out of the cave.

Then I would discover that I was still securely tied up.

I had not escaped.

I got angry with myself.

It was an endless fight, terrible and at the same time wonderful.

"Whether we are children or grownups
we need to know
that
we are totally responsible for our actions.
We are tied with chains.
Chains that we have fashioned ourselves.
If what we are saying
or doing to people adds to their bonds,
then to us
it becomes heavy chains round our necks.
Do we really think
that hurting someone
is a simple thing?"

The Wings

One day at school, the teacher had asked us:

"Had you been able to fly, what you would have liked to be?"

All the kids named the bird they would have liked to be. When my turn came, I said: "A human being."

The teacher gave me a stern look and asked me whether I was stupid.

"Human beings do not fly," he said.

When I mentioned to grandpa the question of the teacher and his answer, he said:

"The spiritual wings of man are the truest, the most beautiful wings of the creation, because Man fashions them himself after a great struggle.

" They have not been given to him.

" He is fighting to create them.

" Feather by feather.

" Thought by thought.

" I have promised to teach you to fly and I will do it."

There was so much confidence and knowledge in his voice and in his eyes, that I did not have any doubt that he would realize his promise.

The next day the other kids at school were sneering at me for my answer.

They were slapping my back, laughing and saying:

"Where are your wings? Open them so we can see them. Stupid! You are Stupid! What an idea; to fly! No one is going to love you as you are, imagine you with wings as well!"

Every single word, every slap, was a knife in my heart.

I have no idea how I managed to remain standing. I was only staring, like frozen, and whishing the earth would open to swallow me maybe this would save me from the pain.

I was losing my faith in myself.

I was losing my faith in people.

I could foresee my future: loneliness, rejection.

Do you know which was my greatest fear those moments and others similar to them?

That I will die alone, frozen from the cold of my heart and the icy north wind, rejected both by all the people and by myself.

The little girl created that image, which, years later and with difficulty, I managed to make her change it.

For years I was trying to hide from my fears perhaps if they couldn't find me, they wouldn't become real. But in time I learned, by fighting them, that they are total cowards. If one dares stand up to them and look them in the eye, feeling strong and decided to win, they disappear.

The more you hide, the higher and the stronger your fears become. They will always wait for you. Running away will not save you.

Stand up and fight them!

You are certain to win.

But that day with the other kids, before having learned all this, I was weeping disconsolate in the arms of my grandpa.

"You are the warrior in your life.
Choose the way by which you will face your fears.
You may regard them as lessons, as illusions,
or you may let them vanquish you.
You have the wisdom to choose what is best for you."

"I don't believe anything of what you are telling me anymore," I was saying between sobs. "I will never be able to fly. People do not fly. What kind of success can I have in my life? They all call me stupid and they are sneering at me for what I am. What can I expect? What can I hope for? I do not believe what you are telling me anymore. Every day I am in pain."

I left the room angry with him and with me, for having dared to hope and hid crying under my bedclothes.

Grandpa did not come to check on how I was faring. I was keeping my ears pealed all the time, hoping to hear his steps, the door opening and him entering to help me overcome the despair I was feeling.

I was surprised that he did not show up at all.

The next day I was thinking, more than anything, grandpa's behaviour. After school, I ran to find him.

"Why did you not come to comfort me?" I asked him.

"Because you left my arms.

" Every time you are making your choices.

" You rejected the warmth and the love I was giving you.

" You decided to remain alone with your pain.

" You should know that, each time, you are going to have what you have chosen.

" This is what you want, this is what you will get. No one will run after you.

" There are around you people who may hurt you, but also, if you want to see it, there are people who love you and want to help you.

" If you choose to be on the side of love and tenderness, you are going to have them.

" If you choose to stay with anger and loneliness as companions, it is your right.

" You are going to live with them. Cruelty will not be coming from the others; you are the one who is going to be cruel and relentless with yourself.

" Make you choice. I am always here, and I love you for what you are.

" Love yourself for what you are today.

" Do not wait for what you are going to become tomorrow. Ask those people who love you no matter what your difficulties are, for help and love.

" You are never alone. You have all of us. If you agree, give me your hand."

I gave him my hand and I put my arms around him.

"Nothing is given in this life, dearest," he went on. "Every moment you are solely responsible for what you are living.

" You can choose love or hate and anger, light or darkness. You can choose joy or sorrow, resignation or battle.

" Nothing is gifted to you in life. Whatever you want, you have to conquer it.

" Wallowing in sorrow and refusing to get out, is a weakness.

" It is ignorance of who you are.

" It is low self-esteem.

" You do not love yourself enough so that you will choose the light."

I couldn't but interrupt him:

"Weak people do not fly, Grandpa?"

> *"When people hurt us,*
>
> *we run like wounded animals to hide in our cave.*
>
> *The treatment to our affliction is to get out into the light*
>
> *and tell someone who loves us what we are in need of.*
>
> *This is not weakness. It is strength.*
>
> *It is transcendence."*

"Cowards do not fly they are held back by their chains.

" Fearful like wild animals, those chained in sunless caves show their teeth to the light.

" You have to choose, right here, right now, who you wish to be.

" Yesterday does not exist; tomorrow does not exist.

" You are living only in the now. You can choose only in the now.

" Do you want to fly?"

"Yes!"

"Even by saying it, you create a responsibility. Do you take the responsibility of your wants?"

"I want to fly."

"I am not preparing you for a world fashioned by angels. I am preparing you to fight.

" To light up, first of all, your darkness.

" It is going to be a difficult battle. It will take long.

" They are going to ridicule you, to doubt you, to sneer at you, to hurt you deeply.

" The first lessons, your first feathers, are given to you by those kids at your school, the ones that they are hurting you today.

" I am preparing you so that you will fashion imperishable wings, which will keep you forever aloft in eternity.

" Aloft, in the clear sky of the soul, within the eternal, inexhaustible source of your origin.

" Nothing less than this.

" Nothing inferior to this."

One day grandpa spoke to me about George Gurgieff.

His Greek name was George Georgiades. He was a Greek Armenian mystic and spiritual teacher.

He introduced the 'Fourth Way' to awakening one's consciousness. His father was of Greek descent and his mother from Alexandropol in Armenia.

"My meeting with Gurgieff," he told me was metaphysical.

I saw him for the first time, quite clearly, in a dream, without having seen him ever before or having heard anything about him. In my dream he was carrying a staff and, as soon as he touched me, my soul whirled into space and time.

" What I felt was powerful, but also scary. I was particularly impressed by his piercing eyes.

" I saw signs that told me that I was going to find out about this man at a trip of mine to India. Indeed, years later, I came to India. I had almost forgotten the dream and the face I had seen in my dreams back then. Yet this is how things came about.

" Because of various strange coincidences, I found myself walking in a narrow alley of a city.

" There, I heard a heavenly music that drew me to it like a magnet. It was issuing from a school where mystic dances of self-awareness were being taught, accompanied by the music of a great teacher.

"Magic is
to live your life happily, thanks to your own efforts.
If they tell you that there is no happiness,
do not believe them.
If they tell you that you cannot succeed
do not believe them.
Each one speaks
only through the things
he has achieved in his life."

I went into the building and found myself in front of a black and white photograph, staring into the piercing eyes of the man I had seen in my dreams.

" Gurgieff had studied civilizations and religions, various systems of internal knowledge and practical application. The 'Fourth Way' he introduced, is the way of the man who lives his life among the people, without having the necessity to withdraw into isolation. He believed that Man lives his life quite instinctively, without being aware of his inner reality. In order to escape from this situation, he needs conscious effort and struggle.

" According to Gurgieff, our behaviour towards the world and towards life is the behaviour of demands. I demand and I take, simply because I am me.

" He believed that Man is an incomplete being, who, unconsciously, falls prey to his automated reactions, which are triggered each time by external stimulants of the moment and by random situations.

" He used to say, however, that we have the ability to trans form our inner self and thus become a complete being. Yet this necessitates not only a struggle but also the will to see the truth. It cannot be done if this prerequisite is absent.

" I told you this story, so that you may see that there are things which escape the limits of what we consider logical. It is a magical, wonderful world, in which, when you want it, the teachers you are in need of appear without being called.

" Therefore, you should never stop wishing to see the truth. Read, listen, pay attention around you!

" Everyone has something to give you.

" There is no need to be someone's follower and to wear the blinkers of authority.

" Create your own truth.

" Do not let anyone pull you down from the ladder you are climbing.

" There are many people above you.

" There are many people below you.

" There are also the cowards who are afraid to climb the first step, because the idea of leaving the security of the earth makes them tremble.

" These are the ones who will endeavour to bring you down, so that you will not be reminding them the measure of their weakness.

" Some will hate you, because you are going on, and they will sneer at you for it.

" These are a different kind of cowards. It is always much easier not to struggle.

" Do not give up. Go on!

" Do not loose heart. Be brave.

" Do not embrace hate. Embrace love.

" Believe that you deserve to succeed.

" Only then you will be able to understand those that are below you, and give them a hand to hold on.

" Only then you will be able to get hold of the hand that is extended to you from higher up.

" This is how we climb the ladder. Getting hold of the hand of each other.

" Who stands at the head of the ladder?

" Whose hand is there, to pull up that long human chain?" Each one of us will give one's own answer.

" Do not be afraid to do it."

And grandpa started telling me a fairy story:

"Are we climbing or descending the ladder?
Do we stay below, looking up?
Do we pull down those we can reach
from the steps they have climbed?
Everything exists in this world.
Let us see who we are at this moment.
We can choose
who we want to be
in the now."

The Wings

The Tree That Was Afraid

Once upon a time, there was a tree that lived at the edge of a great precipice.

It was a beautiful, tall tree with strong roots. But the tree was tormented by great fears. Though it wanted not be fearful.

But every day its heart was batting in terror. It was afraid that it will be uprooted and fall down the cliff.

It was afraid of the torrential rainfall, that it would strip its roots of soil and leave it hanging in mid-air.

It was afraid of the strong wind that was threatening to sweep it off the cliff.

It was afraid of the weight of the birds' nests.

It was trembling and every day it was discovering a different danger that was threatening it.

It had though, a very good friend. The rock.

Many years ago, a bird was carrying a seed in its beak. But, as it was flying by, it dropped the seed. The seed rolled to the edge of the precipice, until it was stopped by the rock. The rock always wanted to have a friend.

The seed took roots, the years passed and the seed grew up to become our tree. The rock was watching it grow, become beautiful and strong, and it was happy. But it was also sad, because its friend, the tree, was so frightened.

Every day it would tell the tree:

"Don't be afraid. You have strong roots. You are strong. You are not going to fall."

But the tree would answer, trembling:

"The wind is strong. The rain the same. One day they will manage to uproot me. I am in great pain every time I hold myself against them, so that they will not pull me down."

It starts weeping. Its branches, in their sorrow, droop lifeless towards the ground. The leaves are turning yellow from their fear and they fall before their time.

The wind takes its weeping and carries it far away.

"What's happening? Who's crying?" ask some saplings.

"Does fear determine your life,
or is it determined by your strength?
What kind of concepts on life
are you feeding to your children?
It is with these that they will grow up
and they will arrange their life.
Do you like these concepts?
Do you think
they will make them happy?"

The older one's answer:

"It is the tree that is afraid."

The rock does not know what else to say to the tree. It feels sorry for its friend. It could have been so happy...

One day, a very strong wind is blowing. The tree starts trembling.

It sheds all its leaves. It remains naked.

"I can no longer bear to be afraid," it says to the rock. "I am going to let myself fall."

"No!' says the rock. "Don't be a coward. Raise your branches. Feel your strong roots deep in the soil. You can make it."

"No. I can struggle no longer. Farewell, my friend."

It gives up itself to the howling wind, to be uprooted without any resistance. The wind does its worst and blows with all its might.

The tree does not think of anything, not even of saving itself.

Its branches are nearly torn off.

It lets them go, without forcing them to stay immovable.

It covers its eyes with a branch and waits for its end.

The wind tries for a long time. It blows with all its power.

It does not manage even to shake the tree. Its roots go deep and are strong.

The wind concedes its defeat. It says to the tree:

"You found the way to defeat me. You do not fight me."

The tree does not believe its ears, but remains immobile. The wind says:

"I admire you. Do you want to be my friend?"

Then the tree opens its eyes. It feels strong. Its pains are gone.

"I do!" it says to the wind.

"I admire you," says the rock to the tree. "You defeated the strong wind."

But the tree continues to be afraid and says:

"The rain will uproot me."

One day, heavy rain starts falling on it. The rain creates rivers, which take the soil and empty it into the ravine.

The tree is thinking that now its end has come. It resigns itself to its destiny.

But as soon as it has calmed down, it thinks:

I want to and I can live happily. I will defeat the rain as I did with the wind.

It spreads its branches and enjoys the rain. It spreads its roots and holds back the soil the rain is washing away. It becomes stronger.

The rain gets heavier and heavier, but the tree is no longer afraid.

The rain says to the tree:

"You have defeated me. Do you want to become friends?" And so they did.

The rock is full of joy for its friend. One day it asks the tree: "Are you happy now?"

"No," says the tree. "The birds add weight to my branches, so they may cause me to fall."

"No, my friend," says the rock. "The birds are bringers of life. Their singing brings joy. It all depends on how you perceive everything that is happening."

One day, a bird, that had its nest among the tree branches, let fall from its beak a seed.

"Fears give birth to fears.
Strength gives birth to strength.
Joy gives birth to joy.
What do you wish to bring to life?"

After a while a tiny tree started sprouting. The tree saw it and got the fright of its life.

"But this one is even lower down the precipice than I am. How is it going to survive?" the tree says to the rock. "Teach it to be as strong as you are," says the rock. "But I am not strong."

"You are, but you have yet to learn how much." This made the tree start thinking.

It saw how much it had achieved. For the first time it was looking down the ravine and it was not frightened.

It was strong.

Now it could see it clearly.

It straightened its trunk.

It spread out its branches.

Its roots were boring deep into the ground.

It started laughing.

Its leaves, strong, beautiful, green, were playing with the wind, with the rain, with the birds...

It says to the tiny tree:

"Be strong.

" Do not be afraid.

" You can achieve anything, if you defeat your fears.

" Be peaceful and serene.

" Life is very beautiful, if you want to see its beauty.

" You can become very happy."

By now, many saplings draw strength for the tree that has become strong.

And they lived happily ever after and so did we, only much better.

The Thoughts

Grandpa was a healer. He used to tell me that there are many teachers who are in this dimension, as well as the ones who have passed to another.

Depending on the level we find ourselves, if we want it very much, they will appear in order to teach us.

Their presence may not be always physical, if they have departed this life, but it may manifest itself through all the stuff they have left behind as their spiritual legacy.

They have left traces of themselves behind. We study them and, if they coincide with the direction we wish to take, we follow them.

At some point, we find still other traces. We study these, too. This is how it goes on through our entire life.

Grandpa believed that there is no such thing as "the one", who knows a certain secret or the sole truth.

There is no need to accumulate literary knowledge in order to find this truth. It is always there, available to anyone.

But because the last place we are going to look is inside us, we may deceive ourselves and think that the truth is hidden somewhere else, outside ourselves.

But the truth is always there, as the light is also always there.

If we do not see it, it is not because it has distanced itself from us, but rather because we have wandered away from it.

The light in our life comes and goes.

We leave it and we return to it.

Every man, my grandpa used to say, is as much a wise one, a healer, a mystic, a teacher, as all of us.

The only difference is as to who is able to perceive it.

Who can break his chains and face the reality.

Who is not afraid to act.

Who has understood who he really is.

What he really is.

"Show compassion to Man," grandpa would say. "Love him."

And went on: "His struggle is difficult. He has to uproot things that are deeply rooted. And this hurts.

" Sympathize with him for it. If he hurts you, it will be because he is also hurting.

" Instead of blaming him, instead of rejecting him, wish him to see the light, to find himself. To be happy. Only then he will not wish to harm anyone. Only then he will find peace and beauty.

" Do not judge him, just listen to him.

" Help him to see that you are both the same."

To people who would come to seek his help, he would say that they themselves will heal their self.

He was only a humble servant of the light, of love, of understanding and of truth.

He would raise his hands in prayer and then place them on the shoulders, the head, or whichever part of the body the energy that needed to flow free once more would lead him.

"Pain is not our natural condition.

We are in pain,

because the life we are living gives us pain.

Or rather, the life we are not living,

the choices,

the mistakes,

the past we won't accept."

"Thought makes one sick, thought heals one," he would say. "Thought is the one that creates each moment your reality. Each thought employs a different symptom in order to manifest itself on the human body.

" But we are not just the physical body. We also have energy bodies.

" First energy is blocked on those and then it is manifested on our physical body.

" We are much more that what we are able to see and witness."

He would talk with people, in order to help them discover the situations they were experiencing and the thoughts they had which made them sicken.

"Today," he would say, "it is necessary, more than ever, to change the way we are thinking and the way we see things around us.

" We say that economic problems lead our life to a dead end and this is what prevents us from being happy.

" This is true in a large part.

On the other hand, however, who is responsible for the existing abundance, which he is feeling, which he is attracting? There are people who have the money that would allow them to live happily and to enjoy all the good things in life, yet they behave as if they are the most abject poor in the world. They carry in them the sense of deprivation.

" It is great to have abundance in all aspects of your life, but you also have to enjoy it, you have to feel happy through this, and you have to give joy also to others who need it.

" Do not grumble all the time, because you do not have even more.

" We all may have what we need, depending on the thoughts we are having.

" How do we see our self in life? In abundance? Can we imagine us? Do we deserve it? What attitude are we having? What kind of body posture?

" Is it perhaps the low appreciation of our worth, the experiences we had as children, the need for grumbling, that make us experience the lack of means?

" Are we using everything we want as a dependence trap or as a challenge to succeed, and through that to learn and to grow?

" What have we been taught? How have we learned to experience what is happening to us. What do we believe about life, our relationships, our cohabiting with our fellow human beings? What do we believe about abundance or deprivation?

" Is it we, or certain others inside us, who determine our thoughts? Our life? Are we experiencing our own reality or the reality of certain others, to whom we shudder even to mention that we do not like it, out of fear of disputing something that is considered indisputable?

"If you wish to heal yourself so that you will be able to fly,
you will find around you all kind of treatments.
Everything is available each moment,
to whom has decided to do it.
If you don't believe it,
try and see whether it is true or not.
But you will need strength.
You will need to focus your attention
on what you want."

" Question everything, and believe it afresh, if you see that it is compatible with you.

" For how long are we going to torment ourselves and wait for various 'saviours' to change our life?

" Only our self can save us. We must understand that we have each other, so that together we will be going on, with love and positive thoughts on life and on Man."

Grandpa was telling me:

"Within the sphere of our existence we are creating energy flows from our thoughts and our actions.

" The energy that we have produced is either positive or negative.

" This energy, de pending on what it is, attracts energies compatible with it.

" Life brings us exactly what we wish for.

" So it is necessary, at each single moment, to be fully conscious of what we are thinking about ourselves and about our desires.

" Many times, we find it impossible to contemplate the notion that our convictions are leading us to a life which does not provide us with joy and happiness.

" But so it is. We are solely responsible for what we are experiencing.

"Even if we are 'good kids', if we are conforming with society's rules, if we are bending over backwards so that everyone is pleased with us, and if everything seems perfect, we still have to ask ourselves a very important question: Are we, ourselves, satisfied with this lot? Are we experiencing the kind of life that we would not wish to change?

" You cannot give love to others, if you do not love yourself. You cannot give joy to others, if you are not happy with what you are doing, with what you are offering.

" What kind of food are you providing at any moment to your energy sphere?

" The thoughts are music.

" What kind of music are you composing today?

" Now?

" Everything in the universe is music.

" Does your sphere feed the negative or the positive energy of the universe?

" Are you strengthening the good or the evil?

" The positive or the negative?

" Each one of us, separately, is responsible for his decision.

" Nothing more, nothing less.

" You should know that everything is your own choice.

" If you knew how significant you are for the change of this world, you would change right this moment.

" One person, by oneself, constitutes the entire world. That person can change the entire world."

"How?" I asked.

"Don't ask me how. Find it yourself. Act, so that you understand. Try by yourself to see whether what I am telling you is true for you.

" Do worthy things.

" Travel the soul's itinerary, so that you may see, listen, understand."

"We acknowledge,

we appreciate ourselves.

We are wonderful, no matter what.

Darkness is not a bad thing.

It is the experience

that leads us to the struggle of the conscious choice."

"What does it mean 'travel the soul's itinerary', Grandpa?"
"It means 'I proceed towards worthy acts'…

" The spiritual progress is the only kind of travel which you can begin whenever you decide to do it.

" You do not need anyone's permission for it, you do not need money for expenses, nor do you leave behind people and things the responsibility of which you have undertaken.

" You do not fly in order to get away from someone or something.

" To fly does not mean that you become isolated and that you are leaving behind you people and situations. On the contrary, you come closer to everyone and to everything.

" You do not see things or people as obligations, but as the choices you have made and which you continue to make every moment.

" You can understand yourself better, but also, through yourself, you are better understanding the others. You comprehend their behaviour, because you draw upon your own experience.

" The soul of all people desires the same things.

" To understand this though, you have to talk to the other with love, looking him straight in the eye.

" I recognize myself in the look of the other person.

" We are all the same; the masks are different.

" Look first behind you own, so that you will be able to look behind the masks of the others."

And as it was his custom, grandpa started telling me one of his fairy tales.

"When you say that you want to fly,
you are taking up a responsibility.
No one will fashion wings for you.
You have to fashion them yourself,
bit of down by bit of down,
feather by feather.
Difficult?
Yes!
Yet, what if you do manage it!"

The Thoughts

The Most Evil Prize in the World

Once upon a time, all the wicked witches of that time decided to have the greatest evil contest that had ever been organized.

The winner would become their queen.

The prize was indeed great and so all kinds of wicked witches from the four corners of the Earth gathered to contest their skills. The best idea on how to enslave all the people on Earth would carry the prize.

Many ideas were proposed and, indeed, they were exceptionally good, that is to say, evil.

But one day they heard the last witch in line saying the following:

"I have listened very carefully to all of you. All the proposed plans are, indeed, wonderfully evil. But I am going to propose to you the most evil of all. We are going to enslave the people without their ever finding it out. The slave, who is aware of his enslavement, will try to free himself and he will always be creating problems for us.

" But if we go with my idea, we will not have to bother with them ever again. The people will be serving evil blindly, without either questions or doubts."

Overjoyed the witches were stamping their feet on the ground, shouting: "Oh you, Most Evil One! Tell us how this can be done!"

"Listen," she said. "As of tonight, each one of us will fashion an invisible sphere made of evil and of enslavement thoughts. You are going to feed daily these spheres with your thoughts, until they grow and acquire life and shape.

" We are going to feed them with the worst stuff we can imagine, with what we want to happen. This sphere and the thought shapes that you will have created and given life, will become the invisible world of every man.

" When you have finished this, I will tell you what we are going to do next."

And then came the day when all the witches presented their creations.

"You have done a wonderfully evil job," said the Most Evil One. "Now that everything is ready, let's start for the neighbouring kingdom. As soon as we arrive, we will throw our spheres over the people. You will cover them from head to toe." And so it was done.

When they came back, the witches said: "Our spheres were not enough to cover the children, too. But we have covered all the grownups."

"Doesn't matter," said the witch. "The children cannot do anything. They are of no account."

172

"The shapes need food," said one of the others. "Who is going to feed them so that they will survive?"

"Wait and see," said the Most Evil One.

Indeed, after a while, the people started hating each other, started stealing, killing, thinking only of themselves and no one else.

Their king declared war to his neighbouring kingdom and enslaved the lot of its citizens.

Loneliness, hate, fear, greed, cruelty, were a few only of the shapes the witches had created, and those shapes were feeding on the deeds and the thoughts of the people and were getting stronger by the minute.

The witches, seeing all this, organized a great festivity.

They asked the Most Evil One how did she come by the idea. She answered: "When many spheres are joined together, the evil gets stronger. One here and one there do not have the same impact as when they are a lot together. In this way the one sphere feeds the other incessantly.

"Malevolence hurts only ourselves
and the children who are growing up with us.
We should not blame anyone
if we dislike the life we are living.
We have to take responsibility for our choices.
Why
are we taking it out on the children?
What
are we teaching them with our behaviour?
What
are we perpetuating?"

" Each person ascribes the blame to the other.

" So he kills him, but always there is someone else.

" Do you know why?

" Because no one sees his own sphere.

" So they hate and they kill each other, producing a lot of food for tough shapes, which in turn are feeding us."

At the other end of the world, the good witches were discussing the problem:

"It is going from bad to worse. The people are now slaves, and they do not know it," said one of them.

"We cannot do anything about them, because only themselves can get rid of the evil witches' spheres," pointed out another.

"But as long as they cannot see what they are doing, there is no hope that they will wish to change," said the third.

"So, are we going to let evil win?" they were asking each other.

"There is one hope left," said one.

"Which?" asked eagerly all the others.

"The children. The evil witches consider them weak and insignificant. They have not covered them up. Now, only they can save the world."

"But how? They grow up with parents who are enslaved within the sphere of the evil witches. What can they do?"

"They can keep the goodness alive, until the grownups see what's happening."

The good witches started speaking, one after the other, trying to solve the problem.

"If we talk to the children, then they will understand that they are not helpless beings, but that they are holding the future of the world, the future of the light inside their pure souls. We will teach them how to see the witches' spheres."

"But even if they can see them, what can they do?

How they can keep the flame alive all by themselves?"

"The children will learn to observe their own self, and themselves they will find out about the world."

"They will find how much power they have!"

"They will help the grownups see clearly that they are enslaved."

"Only then, things will change in the world of each person and in its turn, the entire world will change," they concluded.

" And so it happened.

" The wicked witches were labouring to subject the grownups and the good ones to give power to the children.

" Until now, the battle is won at times by the one side and at times by the other.

" Yet, who will win the war?

I could not help it but interrupt the fairy tale.

"Grandpa, who do you think will win?"

"I think the good will win." "The children?"

"The children and as many of the grownups as they retain their purity and the fire for life, the love for the unknown, the optimism, the strength, the kindness, just like the children.

" The more they are becoming, the surest it is that they will win.

"You can break the single switch.
You cannot break a bunch of them.
Many times
it seems that evil is stronger.
This is a well-masqued lie.
When the good joins forces,
then truth will out."

" But they need to join forces.

" Come with me, I want to show you something."

We walked to the vineyard, from which grandpa was producing the wine our family was consuming.

He cut a switch and gave it to me to break.

"Is it easy to break or difficult?" he asked me.

"Easy," I answered.

He gave me two.

I broke them with a little more difficulty.

He kept adding switches and every time it was increasingly difficult to break them.

Until I had a bunch of switches that I could not, no matter how hard I tried, to break.

"Human beings are like this," said grandpa. "United you cannot break them, but divided you can do whatever you like with them."

"Grandpa, is there a way by which we could protect ourselves from the negative energy?

" How can we fight every day for the good?"

"The good witches said about it: Each morning, when you awake up, shut your eyes and imagine the light of the good embracing you. Sense how nice and how warm you are feeling, basking in light of goodness.

" Thank yourself for what it is doing, no matter what it is, and feel grateful for all the things you have. For the love that sur rounds you, for your parents, your friends, your food, your health, for anything you can think of.

" There are a great many, an infinite number of things we can be grateful for.

" Nothing of what we have can be taken for granted. So, give thanks for what you have.

" Choose to be on the side of the good every single day.

" Fight so that the good will win.

” Work hard so that our numbers will increase, and thus we will remain free and able to liberate and all the others.

” Speak and do good deeds wherever you can.

” Find your purpose in this life.

” Love what you are.

” Love Man.

” Wish and pray for both your own good and the good of humanity, the sub lime good.

” Remember each day that you deserve the best and that you can have it.

” Have dreams about what you wish to achieve and have targets.

” All these are your shield.

” Feel it, strong and impregnable, in your hands.

” Work hard with peace and love for yourself, for the children, for the enslaved and the frightened, for your co-combatants.

” Love is uniting you.

” Find them and join forces.

” One day you will win.”

"The children
will become giants,
when they learn
that they are giants.
The giant inside us grows,
only
while he understands his size."

The Dream

One day, grandpa spoke to me about signs.

"In the road our life is taking," he said, "there are signposts to guide us. You need to train your perception in order to distinguish them.

" Opportunities for success always arrive; you will see them, as long as you are not lost in darkness and pessimism. Then, they will pass you by.

" If you want to have light and love in your life, it is not enough to proclaim it.

" You need to see it; and when it knocks on your door, to open it for it.

" But if you wish to remain where you are, then you will shut your ears and eyes and you will not hear anything.

" Afterwards, of course, you will complain that no one has helped you and that everyone out there is determined to harm you, to downgrade you, to flatten you, to destroy you.

" You are not going to want it, and so you will never have it, the light and the love your heart is yearning for.

" So, learn to recognize the signs that will guide you and which are telling you whether you are on the right path or you should take another.

" We are never alone. Loneliness is a lie."

"Grandpa, what is a 'lie' in Greek?"

"The etymology of the word in classical Greek, according to Plato in Cratylus, is the following: The word is derived from the letter 'ψ' plus the word 'evdos' which means 'sleep of the soul'. In the same Dialogue, Plato also maintains that the word for truth, 'alitheia' is something divine, 'theion' in Greek, and is derived from the words 'ali' + 'theia', meaning the divine movement of the being.

The lie is the opposite of the movement."

Sitting on the floor, on my granny's woven rag rug, I would lift my head and look straight into his eyes, absorbing every word. He was resting his hand on my head and me, being warmed by the fire in the hearth that was generously spreading its warmth throughout the humble room, I was immeasurably happy. That evening I listened to a fairy tale that many times in my later life I was induced to recall.

"No one and for whatever reason
has the power to break our wings.
If we sense
that something like this is happening,
it is because we are resting somewhere on the way,
thinking and getting stronger
because of the experience,
until such time as we will be ready to fly again.
We are invulnerable,
because
by now we know the truth of our power."

"Are we lost into oblivion?
Are we in a state of stagnation?
We are a lie.
Do we seek, remember, act?
We are truth."

The Emptyheaded Youth

Once upon a time, in a faraway city lived a poor young man.

He had a great dream: To travel throughout the entire world and, through his fairy tales, to give joy and hope to all the people who were in need of them. To give food and a warm shelter to people who had neither food nor a place to lay their head.

Yet wherever he would tell of his plans, people made fun of him and asked him how did he think that a poor and insignificant lowlife like himself would accomplish something so great.

"Realize who you are," they used to tell him. "Find a job like everyone else, to make a living, to make some money and forget your grandiose dreams. They are not for you."

They were calling him Empty head, because he was insisting on his dream and he wouldn't listen to anyone.

But eventually they persuaded him.

He abandoned his dream and tried to work, like all the people around him.

At one time he worked as a baker. He liked it at the beginning, but then after a time he got bored and he would leave the loaves half-baked.

Then he became a cobbler. In the beginning he would make handsome and sturdy shoes, but then his work deteriorated and the soles of the shoes would come unstuck after taking a few steps.

He also became a town crier, who at beginning was delivering the announcements with a loud voice. But after a while, you had to bring your ear close to his mouth in order to hear what he had to say.

One day he couldn't bear it any longer and he said to his parents:

"I am unhappy. I want to do what all the others do, but I cannot."

"Give it a rest, my child, and do what everyone around you does. Don't seek things that are beyond you," was his mother's advice.

The youth left the house to get some air he thought he would suffocate.

He walked a long way from his home. On the road he met a beggar.

"I am dying of hunger," he told the youth.

"To do something we do not like just for the money
we are going to get,
will not give us happiness.
Everything remains here on Earth.
Truths are the only things we are going to take with us."

Emptyhead fished out of his pocket the last of his money and gave them to the beggar.

Said the beggar:

"The one who listens to the whispers of the soul wins happiness in his life."

And he disappeared...

Emptyhead was confounded by the beggar and his words, which sounded as an answer to his questions.

He returned home and said:

"I am leaving. I am going to win happiness."

"The more you are running after happiness," said his mother, "the further it gets."

"I don't believe in this," said Emptyhead.

"I am leaving."

"But you don't have any money," said she. "Where will you go, my child? You will die on the way."

He wouldn't listen. He took a loaf of bread and a few olives and left.

He took to the road and walked on and on, uphill and down dale. Tired and hungry he arrived before a beautiful castle.

Two guards, sword in hand, asked him:

"Stranger, what has brought you here?"

"I am trying to find happiness," he said.

"We will ask you one question. If you answer it, you can go in."

"I am listening," said Emptyhead.

"What do you need to know, first of all, in order to find happiness?"

Emptyhead thought and thought, but nothing would come to his mind.

"I do not know the answer," he said. "But, please, give me another chance. Ask me another question."

They did not want to, but after his pleading they accepted. So, they asked him:

"What is the meaning of the word 'freedom'?"

What could he say, when this time he did not know what to answer either?

He thanked the guards and left his heart heavy.

I am worthless, he was thinking. I am a poor stupid man. A dreamer. They were right those who were telling me off. How did I dare think, hope, that I would ever achieve something so big? He got angry with himself that he had even thought, that he had dared dream of something like this. The others knew much more about me, than I do about myself, he was musing.

Miserable, ragged, hungry, he was begging, dragging his wretched body from place to place.

He was begging alms from the passers-by. But the coppers they were giving him were not enough to buy food with.

He arrived to a city, where he would eat of the food the citizens were throwing to the dogs.

This is what I deserve, he was thinking.

One day, as he was sitting against the wall of a ruined house, with hand extended in begging and with a resigned look in his face, a little child approached him.

"*What does freedom, plenty, love, purpose,*
soul, life, human being
means to us?
No one is going to ask us these questions
in order to permit us entrance to his kingdom.
We pose these questions to ourselves,
if we want to create our own paradise."

"Is it nice being a beggar?" he asked him. "My parents have no money and they want to send me on the street to beg from the passers-by. But I don't like it. I have other dreams."

In the child's words Emptyhead saw himself.

Suddenly he wanted to say to the child:

"No, strive to achieve your dreams. Don't force yourself to do something, because the others want you to. See how low I have fallen."

He started weeping and he went on weeping until all the bitterness was washed away from inside him.

The next day the child came back.

Emptyhead started talking to him through fairy tale s and, at the same time, he was recounting them for the benefit of the child inside him.

He remembered the words of that strange beggar.

The whisperings of the soul were telling him to strive for his dream.

He started to tell stories, without being afraid.

Every day, more and more people were gathering around him.

They were giving him money. Now he could eat, buy clothes, have a house to stay. He could even give some to the child, his first friend, to aid him make of his own dream a reality.

He became the best storyteller of the country.

His fame reached even the king.

The king invited him to the palace.

Emptyhead went there and told the king many beautiful fairy tales.

The king was delighted. He did not want to let him leave. He wanted to keep him at the palace, to exclusively enjoy his storytelling.

"You can have all the wealth your soul may desire," he told him.

"I am sorry, my King, but I do not want to do this," he answered.

"Then, I will cut off your head!"

Emptyhead, quite calmly, answered:

"You are the King and you may do as you wish. But, if you want, let me tell you a last fairy tale."

Full of curiosity, the king sat down to listen. And so, our storyteller started recounting:

"Once upon a time, there was a king. He was living happily in his kingdom, with his wife and a daughter. He was just, kind, and loved by everyone.

" But one day, a wicked witch got envious of the king's kind ness and the happiness of his people. Having shifted her shape to that of a man, she presented herself to the king and said:

" 'The fame of your kindness has reached to the ends of the Earth. My king sends you this crown. If you wear it constantly and never remove it, you will remain for ever young."

" The king was dazzled by the crown's richness and beauty. He put it on straight away.

" But from that moment on, he became a different person. He started wanting to own everything.

" He wanted to shut up all the birds in cages, so that they would sing only for him. Those he could not catch, he was killing them.

"Don't you ever let anyone
or anything
pull you down from the step you have conquered.
You may fall easily,
but climbing up is difficult."

He would incarcerate or kill whoever said anything different than what he was saying.

" The happy kingdom changed. It was enveloped in dark ness, sadness and misery. The people, the animals, the birds, the trees were dying daily.

" And the king, with the magical crown on his head, saw it all and none of it affected him he was only thinking how he could make everything his own.

" One day, his daughter fell seriously ill a decline for which her extreme sadness was to blame.

" No one could affect a cure. The king sent town criers everywhere. 'Whoever cures the king's daughter, the king will pay him with bagful of gold!'

" The days were passing. No one showed up. They were all afraid of failure and of the king.

" The king was in despair that he might lose his only child.

" He sent out new town criers: 'Whoever cures my daughter will be given the crown that never leaves my head. I give up my youth, so that my daughter may live!'

" After a while, a good wizard arrived. He cured the princess. The king took off his crown and gave it to him. And then, all of a sudden, he awoke up from his lethargy! He did not know what had transpired all this time, or what he had done himself.

" Says the wizard: 'The spells would come undone only if you, yourself, take this, precious for you crown, from your head, for the sake of love.'

" They threw the crown down the bottomless ravine of a three peaked enchanted mountain, as the wizard directed them, and they lived happily ever after."

The king immediately realized what the storyteller wanted to convey to him and he let him go, on condition that whenever he would call him, he would come to the palace to tell him stories.

And so life was going on.

Until a day when the king's daughter saw the storyteller. The two young people fell in love.

Emptyhead went to her father and told him that he loved the princess and wanted to marry her.

The king, aghast at his effrontery, thought of cutting off Emptyhead's head, but then he had the idea to fool him by sending him to places from which he would not be able to return.

And so he said to him: "I will give you my daughter to wife, if you bring me a crown worthy of a king like myself."

The king, sure of having got rid of Emptyhead, he was thinking of him and was laughing at his stupidity.

If he ever came back, he was going to tell him that the crown was not precious enough and so he would neither give him his daughter nor he would be deprived of the fairy tales he liked so much.

No matter what, he would come on the winning side.

So, in the evening, when Emptyhead came back, the king believed that the young man had given up and got ready to listen to yet another fairy tale.

But Emptyhead greeted him calmly and said: "My King, I have brought what you have asked of me," and he brought out of his bag a crown of myrtle.

"Do we wish

to be crowned with the spectacular

and the transient or with the humble and eternal?

Everything is the result of our choices and decisions

which we are making every moment,

always with respect towards ourselves and the others."

"What's this?" shouted the king, purple with anger.

"My King," said Emptyhead, "you asked for something that it is worthy for a king such as yourself. Your kindness, your wisdom, your humility are creating the most precious crown on Earth. These are eternal, as those myrtle branches are, too. Only these are fit for a king such as yourself."

The king thought hard and long and, realizing the Emptyhead was right, gave him his daughter to wife.

Emptyhead lived very happily and he became a king who was always doing good deeds.

He helped many children realize their dreams and, in that kingdom, no one was ever hungry.

And they lived happily ever after, and we did even better.

"All our wealth will remain here.
We will take with us
only the experience of love.
We cannot fly carrying heavier baggage.
We are going to stay down
until we realize it."

The Creation

"Grandpa, what is the answer to the questions Emptyhead did not answer?"

"The answer to the first question, you will find it yourself," he told me. "The second was what is the meaning of the word 'freedom'. The etymology of the word in Greek comes from 'eléfthyn òpou erà'. It means 'one goes wherever he wishes to'."

"Are people free, Grandpa?" I asked.

"A man can be free only when he is telling the truth to himself on whether he is free or not. I am, I going where I wish to go? Or am I a slave?"

"Whose slave?"

"The word for 'slave' is 'doùlos' and is derived from the verb 'dèo', which means 'I tie up'. Whose slave would Emptyhead become, were he to stay at the palace when the king threatened to kill him?"

"Of fear."

"So the man who is not free, he is the slave of fear. Because, however, the bonds are invisible, we cannot see them."

"How can we see them, when they are invisible?"

"When we turn the whisperings of our soul into a loud voice. Then we will awake up and we will see them.

" But for this to happen, we need first to know our self.

" To speak the truth.

" The truth is the one which awakes us up; the lie puts us to sleep."

"So, Grandpa, the answer to the question, how are we going to find happiness, is to know what we want, to believe that we deserve to have it, to work for it, and to believe that happiness exists and it is not going away from us."

Grandpa happily agreed with me.

For days afterwards, I kept thinking grandpa's story.

I told him that I was wondering about something:

"But Emptyhead lost that beautiful castle where he first came to."

"Had Emptyhead stayed to weep outside the castle he had lost, then he may not have achieved anything of all the things he achieved in his life, and he may even have died of the cold.

" He did not know yet himself at that moment, he did not yet have the power to take his decisions. But he went on forward and found happiness.

" In life, we find everything inside us.

" We are giving life with every thought and every decision either towards the negative or towards the positive.

" The energy of our thoughts and our convictions creates our reality every single moment.

" The guards were not to blame. The king of the castle was not to blame for putting the questions.

Emptyhead was not to blame either, because, until that moment, this was what he believed himself to be.

" Do you remember the little bird that we saved, just before the cat would grab it, when it fell from its nest under the eaves? Should it have been punished because it fell?

"We can blame no one,

if we decide to spend our time weeping

because we have been denied something,

which we are considering our sole chance for happiness.

We are all the chances.

Everything develops inside us."

" It had a really valid excuse for the difficult position it found itself:

" It had not yet learned to fly.

" But when we have learned to fly, we are responsible as to how we are living our life.

" Life is vibrations. The energy, which we are creating within our sphere, is vibrations that affect the things we are attracting. Thoughts of malevolence, of envy, will return back to us, as vibrations, and they will realize a corresponding reality. Thoughts of kindness, of love, will come back to us, as reality.

" In classical Greek the word 'fthònos', meaning 'envy' is de rived from the verb 'fthìno', meaning 'being reduced'.

" A person having thoughts of envy and jealousy may be made ill by their energy, because it reduces the positive energy and strengthens the negative, which, in its turn, attacks that person and no one else.

" Therefore, if you wish harm upon someone, you are essentially attracting the evil upon you, because it is established within your sphere.

" You are the one who is nurturing it, you are the one who is giving it power, and eventually it will become so powerful that it also eats you up.

" The more negative are our thoughts, the lower frequencies we are emitting.

" This, in its turn, leads to the creation of even more frightful thought shapes, which dominate us.

" You are totally responsible for the life you are creating.

" You are the creator of your life.

" Do not hold responsible for it parents, siblings, friends, comrades, collaborators, bosses, known or unknown people.

" Every moment you are creating your world and this world of yours affects the overall conscientiousness of humanity.

" For me, this is the truth. If it is also for you, I ask you to investigate it. To experiment with yourself and the function of life.

" Before you answer, search, investigate, think well. Question everything everywhere, and give new answers."

Once in my life, I found myself in a distant land. I was seeking the truth about myself.

In this my quest, I heard speaking about a man, whom everyone called wise and who could foretell the future.

I requested to be taken to him and indeed I was.

He was a thin, kind looking old man, with wonderful eyes.

He greeted me cordially.

"Why have you come to me?" he asked.

"I am feeling fearful and insecure about life. I would like to know the future," I told him.

He asked me to give him my hand.

He took it between his two palms and he shut his eyes.

I was anxious to hear what he had to tell me.

I was thinking, what should I do in case he sees that I am not worthy enough to succeed?

That I am not sufficient for what I want?

Finally, he spoke, and he said:

"What you want and you believe that will happen, will happen exactly as per your wishes."

"The thoughts
of jealousy, envy, anger, guilt,
emit low frequency vibrations, which result in sickness.
If we do not wish to suffer tomorrow,
we need to heal ourselves today."

193

I did not expect this answer.

I preferred the future to have written the script for my account.

This answer was imposing upon me responsibilities.

I was quite upset and I never forgot his words. They kept shaking me awake. They were reminding me what I should never ever forget.

I am my life and I have sole responsibility for it.

As I was going away, he said after me:

"Existence does need you."

Existence needs every single one of us.

We are all equally important and loved. So much the same that the mind cannot comprehend it. So it is in it that we are divided, separated.

We become important and unimportant beings.

Important person is considered to be the educated one, the rich, the powerful.

Unimportant are all the others, because of colour, religion, country, poverty, kind of work undertaken.

Freedom of expression means I respect who you are and what you believe in.

Nothing can be changed through ridicule and violence.

Violence generates violence.

Let us say that we are able to kill all those we believe that they believe in wrong ideas.

What will happen?

Who will remain alive?

Is such a thing possible?

We only need to connect with our spirit, through the channel of love, which joins us all.

Only then we will be aware of the truth.

Only then.

Do you know why I am writing you this letter?

Because I love life.

I love Man

In this way we are talking, as we could not have ever done it otherwise.

We are connecting with each other.

In my lifetime I have lived moments of darkness and moments of the glory of Man.

I saw those virtual spheres trample people in order to save themselves, I saw hundreds of thousands of people put to death by strong spheres of power whose aim was the gain and the prevalence of their ideas.

I saw people leading armies in the name of freedom, to kill entire people, for their own good, as they were saying.

I saw the hypocrisy, I saw... I saw... At some point I could not take it any longer.

I admitted that the negative force spheres rule this world.

What should I fight for?

Which love could I speak of?

Which light?

I gave up...

"If we believe
that in this life it is not worth it
to fight for the good,
we should know
that this is what they want us to believe.
Who are 'they'?
We will find out if we search for them."

I persuaded myself that, in this life and people's nature being granted, there is nothing worth striving for.

No one can fly.

Grandpa was wrong.

 Only my teacher was right.

Not myself... Not anyone.

This is what the spheres were also telling me.

"Give up.

" This is the world; it's not worth it.

" Give up!

" Can't you see, can't you hear what's going on?

" They are ridiculing you.

" Listen to us.

" It's for your own good we are telling you this.

" Give up!

" It makes no sense.

 " It makes no sense to fight.

 " It makes no sense to hope.

" Man is not worth it.

" Give up!

 " Be silent.

" Sleep.

" Take in your arms the mobile, the computer, the T.V. and sleep sweetly and nicely.

" Be silent.

 " Rest.

" We will tell you what to believe.

 " Don't tire yourself thinking.

" We know better.

" The size of your mind is such that you should not be tiring it by thinking.

 " Rest. Sleep."

And indeed, I slept for several years.

What did awake me up?

A terrible pain at the corners of my eyes and in my heart was what awoke me up.

They were the dreams that were being crushed, were melting inside me, and were turned into bitter tears.

This is what awoke me up, but also grandpa's words.

"Whatever happens in our life happens at its right time. It is the right spiritual moment for our development. It is the completion of a knowledge cycle, of a conscious desire."

Grandpa was right.

There comes indeed a magic moment, when things that you desire happen things for which you have worked.

If you take account of your life, you will see a magical script, in which all things fasten upon each other working rather like cogwheels so that you have the kind of life you want.

Whether you like it or not.

It is you the one who determined it.

Every moment in our life is important, because we are creating things.

Life is very interesting and beautiful.

"Grab today's chance
to make your dreams come true.
You are powerful.
You are a wonderful being.
Find your own truth,
and everything may be changed."

The Gratitude

Grandpa told me once that there was something I should not ever forget.

When I asked him what was that something, he said:

"The cup."

"What does a cup have to do with life?" I asked, laughing.

"Listen and you will understand," he said. "Around 580 B.C. a very important Greek philosopher, mathematician, geometer, music theorist and the founder of Greek mathematics was born. Pythagoras.

" So, Pythagoras, in order to teach both himself and his pupils, fashioned a clay cup for drinking wine. This cup would empty itself, in a magical way, if the one holding it were proven greedy.

" It was a hydraulic gadget, which on the inside had a line at some distance from the rim.

" If, when pouring in wine, you went over the line, then the cup emptied itself, through a secret hole at its base.

" The cup is dated at the 6th century B.C. and it is a masterpiece of the hydraulic technology and the knowledge of the ancient Greeks.

"It was called also 'the just cup', because Pythagoras, by creating it, wanted to teach us that we need to remember every single moment that if we overstep the limits, we become greedy and we are not going to lose only what lies beyond that limit, but also all that we have accumulated up to that moment."

"How am I going to recognize that limit, Grandpa, without any lines to see, such as Pythagoras' cup had?" I asked.

"No one else but yourself can put limits to what you want. When you will get to know yourself, then you will know.

"What I am telling you is that you should enjoy what you are given every day.

"If you are spending all your thoughts and energy in how you are going to acquire more of anything, you will find yourself at some point with the dismal realization that you have spent your life in worthless things and thoughts.

" And now I want to talk to you about another Greek philosopher. He was Diogenes of Sinope, and lived in 400423 B.C.

" People called him 'kyon', meaning 'dog', because he was the main representative of the cynic philosophy, which had as its emblem a dog 'kyna', in classical Greek.

" It was a school of philosophy which despised dogmas, material needs, authorities all the things that enslave a man.

" Diogenes used puns and jokes in his teaching.

" He lived into a large clay jar, which he rolled here and there, to show that we do not have a real need even for a house.

" He used to say: 'I see a lot of people competing, running this way and that, but I do not see anyone fighting for the acquirement of virtue.'

One day, it was high noon, he lit a lamp and, carrying it, went round the streets.

" When people asked him what was he doing, he said: 'I am searching for a human being.'

"Let us get rid of the burdens we are carrying,
in order to heal the wounds on our shoulders.
There we will attach our wings.
Strong wings, so that we may fly high.
We can do it."

"Another time, he was sitting under a statue and, with arm extended, he was begging it for alms.

" When the surprised passers-by asked him what was he doing, he answered:

'I am practising not to be disappointed by the people's insensibility.'"

And now, I will follow Pythagoras' advice, who said:

"Do not say a little with many words, but a lot with a few words." I am ending this letter here.

But I will also follow with a saying of Diogenes when he was told that, "You are old now. Get some rest", and he answered: "Were I was taking part in a foot race, should I relax towards the end instead of accelerating?

" So I will accelerate, too, and I will start, straight away, to write my next letter to you.

I wish that you would all be of good health.

Until we meet again, may Light,
Love, and Gratitude fill each moment of your life.

My love to you all,

Donysia

P.S. And a last word from Pythagoras: "The great science of living happily is to live in the present."

"Existence needs us today.
Not tomorrow.
Today.
Now.
The trip of life is real,
only when it goes towards worthy aims."

BIOGRAPHICAL NOTE

Dionysia Therianou was born in 1965, in Zakynthos, Greece.

She studied accounting and after graduation she travelled as a volunteer, responsible for a development programme, to Cameroon in Africa. Following this powerful life experience, she returned to her island, where she worked as an accountant and as a teacher in accounting. At the same time, however, her quest for self-awareness and for getting to know the world took her to far-off places. She travelled to philosophical centres around the world, spoke with many people – ordinary, illiterate, educated, wise, outcasts of their own self and of society, children, grown-ups, of all races and colours. All these years, in order to be able to communicate with as many people as possible, she taught herself, through books, foreign languages and so today she can speak English, French, Italian, and now she is teaching herself Spanish.

Being profoundly aware of the responsibility of her existence and of the truth towards one's self, Dionysia reached a moment when she decided to give voice to the whispers of her soul and so quitted accounting.

She turned to writing, to painting and ceramic-making.

She is working in the family business – the family estate of agrotourism and organic farming – she paints and creates handicrafts.

Part of her great, holy dream has become reality with the publication of this book you are reading.

Printed in Great Britain
by Amazon

79480814R00122